Archbishop of York

Sermons Preached on the Evening of Each Wednesday and Friday

During the Season of Lent in the Church of St. Mary-the-Virgin, Oxford

Archbishop of York

Sermons Preached on the Evening of Each Wednesday and Friday
During the Season of Lent in the Church of St. Mary-the-Virgin, Oxford

ISBN/EAN: 9783744719643

Printed in Europe, USA, Canada, Australia, Japan

Cover: Foto ©Lupo / pixelio.de

More available books at **www.hansebooks.com**

The Ministration of the Spirit.

SERMONS

PREACHED ON

THE EVENING OF EACH WEDNESDAY AND FRIDAY

DURING

The Season of Lent,

IN THE

CHURCH OF ST. MARY-THE-VIRGIN, OXFORD.

BY

THE LORD ARCHBISHOP OF YORK.   THE LORD BISHOP OF LONDON.
PROFESSOR MANSEL.   J. R. WOODFORD, M.A.
CHR. WORDSWORTH, D.D.   E. B. PUSEY, D.D.
T. L. CLAUGHTON, M.A.   DANIEL MOORE, M.A.
A. P. STANLEY, D.D.   W. C. MAGEE, D.D.
T. T. CARTER, M.A.   THE DEAN OF CANTERBURY.

WITH A PREFACE

BY

SAMUEL, LORD BISHOP OF OXFORD.

Oxford,
AND 377, STRAND, LONDON:
JOHN HENRY AND JAMES PARKER.
1863.

Printed by Messrs. Parker, Cornmarket, Oxford.

PREFACE.

THE Sermons comprised in this volume were preached at St. Mary's Church on the Wednesdays and Fridays of Lent, 1863, according to a custom now of some years standing, by preachers appointed by myself. Each one of this annual series of Sermons has dealt in detail with some great verity of Christian doctrine, or some important feature of the Christian life. But amongst all of these no subject is of deeper moment than that which has occupied the preachers of this year, nor is there any one upon which the special dangers of the present time make a calm earnest statement and a devout consideration of its great features more important.

May it please God to give His blessing to this attempt to set forth His truth.

S. OXON.

CUDDESDON PALACE,
May, 1863.

CONTENTS.

SERMON I.
The Abiding Presence of the Spirit in the Church, the Fulfilment of Christ's Promise.
By THE LORD ARCHBISHOP OF YORK.

SERMON II.
The Spirit, a Divine Person, to be Worshipped and Glorified.
By H. L. MANSEL, B.D.

SERMON III.
The Spirit, the Teacher of the Church.
By CHR. WORDSWORTH, D.D.

SERMON IV.
The Spirit, the Giver of Life.
By T. L. CLAUGHTON, M.A.

SERMON V.
The Grieving of the Spirit.
By A. P. STANLEY, D.D.

SERMON VI.
The Sin against the Holy Ghost.
By T. T. CARTER, M.A.

SERMON VII.

The Spirit convincing of Sin.

By THE LORD BISHOP OF LONDON.

SERMON VIII.

The Spirit interceding.

By J. R. WOODFORD, M.A.

SERMON IX.

The Spirit comforting.

By E. B. PUSEY, D.D.

SERMON X.

The Spirit witnessing with our spirit.

By DANIEL MOORE, M.A.

SERMON XI.

Growth in Grace.

By W. C. MAGEE, D.D.

SERMON XII.

The Perfected Work of the Spirit.

By THE VERY REV. THE DEAN OF CANTERBURY.

SERMON I.

The Abiding Presence of the Spirit in the Church, the Fulfilment of Christ's Promise.

BY

THE LORD ARCHBISHOP OF YORK.

The Abiding Presence of the Spirit in the Church, the Fulfilment of Christ's Promise.

JOHN xvi. 7.

"Nevertheless I tell you the truth; It is expedient for you that I go away: for if I go not away, the Comforter will not come unto you; but if I depart, I will send Him unto you."

THESE words were addressed to the twelve whom it had been the principal work of Jesus to train for the ministry of His Church. And He had trained them through many long months of constant and close companionship. He had taught them not by a measured hour of formal teaching, but by admitting them into the inmost circle of His life. All that little band, Master and scholars, had hungered and thirsted together, and wandered on the shores and hill-slopes of Galilee, till their feet were weary. They had shared the admiration of the people in common; in common had been asked to depart out of their coasts. He had studied every shade and change of their character, as the daily accidents of life played over them, as the strong sun had looked down on the Sea of Galilee, now bright as glass, now rippled by the breeze, now beaten into storm. And in every emergency He had been nigh to guide them. Their foolish pride and rivalry, their halting doubts and weak despondency, had been treated with the medicine that best suited each. And they basked in the light of His presence; thought with His thoughts, and moulded themselves on the pattern of His life; cared not for food or raiment, being sure that He would clothe and feed them; leaned on the strong staff of His counsel, and felt, in all better moments at least, that they were safe. Something of this we all know, and yet perhaps we may not have fully perceived how large a share this plan of education for the disciples occupied in His ministry; how He trained *them* rather than taught the people; how He unfolded His doctrines in succession as they could bear them best; how the communion they enjoyed already with the Lord was the type of His union with His Church.

And now these twelve are told that He must leave them. More: they are assured that it is expedient for them that He should go away. How, they ask themselves, could it be expedient for them to lose their Friend, their Counsellor, their Head, their Life? What could they have in exchange for Jesus, the Christ of God, that would not leave them a balance of irreparable loss? And so these words seemed to them the most difficult of the words of Jesus. They brought the disciples to the verge of a deep mystery of God, that it was in some way essential to the growth of the Church and to the growth of Christian life in their individual hearts, that their Lord should ascend where He was before, and the work that He had begun should be carried on by another. Another, yet not another! No longer Christ visible in the flesh, but Christ dwelling in them by His Spirit, was the power that was to conquer evil and renew them to salvation. They could not understand it; nor can we. We cannot tell why the Lord tarried but a few years in His tabernacle of flesh, why the Church at Pentecost should be founded, when His visible presence had been already withdrawn; but thus much at least we know, that Christ by His Spirit has ever been present with His Church; that He is now present with us by the same Spirit, in a true and literal sense; that the tokens of His working are manifold; and that we may reckon on His presence and comfort to the end.

I. All that tender care and loving nurture of the Apostles failed to make them know their Lord. Their last words almost were to doubt His prophecy about His sufferings, their last act almost was to flee from His side. Some mighty power must have intervened between the time when they shrank from their Master, faint of heart and blunt of apprehension, and the time when they stood up before rulers and kings, and with clear speech and high courage set forth the way of life. The transformation was too great to be accounted for as the reaction of their own thoughts; it was not shame, nor the conviction of sin, nor further study, nor pressure from without, that turned them from the timid companions to the brave messengers of the Lord. Such causes would have operated as favourably whilst their Lord was present with them. If we passed through a forest where we had once been before, and saw the trees cleared away from a particular spot, and instead of their umbrage the sunlight streaming down upon the open, and instead of fungus and bracken the young shoots of corn sparkling in ranks over the field, we should say without the smallest doubt, Here man's hand has been, and left these marks of cultivation. And so it is legitimate to say, comparing the Peter of the Acts with the Peter of the Gospel, or the Paul that preached at Corinth with the Paul who persecuted at Jerusalem, that God's hand has been there, felling the old stocks of tradition and digging out their roots, letting in the new light and breath of heaven, and planting good seed for future fruit. Whatever may be the case now, nothing is more fair to say, more certain to believe, than that there was even an accession of power and energy in the work of Christ after He Himself had left it and committed it to the Holy Spirit. It was even expedient for a Paul or a Peter that Christ should go away, and the Comforter should come. Not that this implies a comparison and rivalry between two, but that His going away, and the mode of that going, were the sources of new power over evil. It is rather a comparison between the Lord in His human pilgrimage, straitened and pained till He should have been baptized with the baptism of suffering, and the Lord when He had paid the ransom of sin, triumphed over death, and begun to intercede in heaven for those whom He loved. It was expedient that the march of God's purpose should not be arrested in any of its steps—agony, suffering, death, resurrection, ascension; and therefore it was expedient that Jesus should depart. But study well, I beg of you, the greatness of that transformation of human souls; and say whether it was wrought by any other power than that of the present God.

And now turn to the other form of the same work, the growth of the Church on earth in the face of every kind of danger. Go back, if you will, to the year of salvation 64, when Rome, the queen city of the world, was almost burnt to ashes, and the Christians were denounced to an exasperated people as guilty of that desolation. What more could be needed for the destruction of Christianity? The Christians shall be dragged out of every hiding-place, and imagination shall be taxed to find new modes of death for them. Who could believe that through this storm of hatred the frail bark of the Church could ride safe? Those that escaped the sword and flame, must yield to the moral torture of the universal abhorrence of men. Yet through that persecution, and many another as fierce, the faith of Christ remained on the earth; nay, grew and prospered on that which would have shipwrecked any worldly institution. The martyred blood and ashes, to use our own poet's well-known image, were like seed sown which bare fruit a hundredfold. And when we question our histories as to the causes of the success of the Gospel, and receive from them this and that partial answer, the very insufficiency of all these answers put together proves that without the one cause—the power of God working in and with the Gospel—we have no account to give of so great a phenomenon.

II. And what is it that now strikes sadness into many a religious mind? Is it not the latent fear that the fire which once burnt shines for us no more? A religion, to be a support to us, must bring us near to God's presence. To me it would be nothing that you should point to heaven and say, 'Far off, beyond yon screen of shining stars, is the eternal throne, where He sits in an atmosphere of light, and glory, and praises.' Is not the answer ready? 'The God I need is not a God that dwells afar off, whom I am to know through books and discourses, but One that will be near me always, giving me refuge under the shadow of His wings from all terror; one who will lift me up to feelings of love, to efforts of duty, of which I thought my nature incapable. More blessed it were to walk for one half-hour by the side of the Sea of Tiberias, to listen to a present Saviour's living words, than a whole life of a religion of history and disquisition, which is in effect no better than a banishment from God.'

And this is the kind of feeling which has driven

many to seek the Divine presence by ways of their own devising,—by great religious excitement, by forming new sects and unions, in the hope that into the new body a new spirit may descend. This has given power to those impostors who offer new books of revelation, or profess to commune directly with the world of spirits. There is in all who know the power of religion at all the wish to live before the presence of God; they are drawn towards Him, and yearn to be near Him, and so much the more, the more their religion is sincere. And yet this state of dejection, or of wild searching after new religious manifestations, seems to overlook the promises of our Lord when the Comforter was sent. The Comforter was to abide with us for ever; and His functions were to benefit the Church perpetually. For ever He was to convince the world of sin, and righteousness, and judgment; of its own sin and Christ's righteousness, and the judgment of God that shall be hereafter. There was no day fixed at which He should cease to testify of Christ, to bring all things to our remembrance that Christ has said, to intercede for us, to comfort us. Whatever be the present state of the Church, Christ promised beyond all doubt that the life and power of the Spirit should be with it for ever. There must be then the same vitality, the same power of growth in the Church; there must be the same life-blood to quicken our hearts, as that which made Paul strong in the faith, and sustained the courage of a Stephen, or a Polycarp at the stake. And before we admit even to ourselves that Christianity is a growth of the past, which has left to us only its withering leaves and hollow trunk, let us reverently ask whether God is not present now, as of old, to help, to comfort, to renew us. Let us examine well the tokens of His presence; and if Christ be still "God with us," let us banish our doubts and fall down before Him, and say with one that doubted, "My Lord and my God!"

III. This age has little to tell of the splendid triumphs of the Gospel over whole countries; although our missions have their fruit, and the promise even of fruit more abundant. But it is not to India, or New Zealand, or Madagascar that we need go for examples of the power of the Holy Spirit over the world of evil. Its evidences are all about us and within us. That even one man should be turned from the power of Satan unto God, would be as clear a proof of Divine intervention, as was the raising of a Lazarus from the grave. But when thousands and tens of thousands are feeling and owning the Spirit's working within them as a fact that cannot be gainsaid, we ought to marvel that we could ever have doubted of His presence. He convinces of sin: daily the Word of God comes home with a terrible power to some stricken heart, and points to the gulf that divides sin from godliness. Daily some soul, shuddering with the felt leprosy of sin, comes to God praying for deliverance. He teaches: and the venerable words of Scripture, obscure because so familiar, flash out with all their meaning upon some prepared soul. He comforts: and after the sense of estrangement from God comes the sweet hope of reconciliation. "The Spirit itself beareth witness with our spirit that we are the children of God." And taught by Him, many a mind draws waters of comfort even out of the stony rocks of adversity; lays aside ease and pleasure that it may do something for God; loves the good with increasing affection; hates sin more than it hates bodily death; would be willing that God should purge out of it every worldly lust and wish; desires to know and live by the truth. And thus the fruit of the Spirit amongst us is the sense of sin, the love of our Father, a belief in a higher world, and the transformation and renewal of our mind by the Holy Ghost, our own will constantly recognising and going along with His work. Facts such as these are not chronicled in newspapers, cannot be reduced to a money value, cannot be debated on in Parliament, or suggest nice points for forensic acuteness. But they are facts. Over ten thousand parishes in England this kind of work is done daily. Who then shall say that Christ our Master is not with His disciples still?

Now all this seems trite and obvious. But yet I do not know any one subject more suitable for a season of more solemn meditation, and for a place like Oxford. We are told, and we have accorded it a too ready belief, that amongst the more cultivated minds the work of the ministry has lost its savour; that we shall see fewer and fewer men of powerful minds willing to devote themselves to the task of preaching the Gospel to Christ's people, because of some notion that that work has lost its reality, and is rather a tradition of a Divine operation than a Divine operation actually going on. And when such a state of things is believed to exist, the belief promotes and fosters it. Let it be admitted, however, that in some cases there is a feeling that the machinery of the Church is less strongly impelled by the force of the Divine Spirit; and how shall such a feeling be met? Let us appeal from the tribunal that pronounces the decision, so crude, so hasty, so half-sighted. Let us appeal from the clever journalist, with his quips and jokes about long services and sermons all too soothing, to the Bible-reading men and women of England, to whom God's Word is a law, whether interpreted tamely or by the most lively eloquence. Let us appeal from the critic in his closet, who perhaps never apprehends one truth but his subtle mind suggests with it six objections, to the practical evidence of those who shape their whole life and stake their whole prospects upon the truth of God's Word and of the hopes it holds out to them. Let us appeal from literary criticism (which yet I would not undervalue) to the test of results; to the humility, and forbearance, and chastity, and brotherly love, and sense of dependence on God produced in Christian minds by the Gospel; to the respect for law and order; to the sanctity of family life; to the good-will between classes, which it has been the means of diffusing through society. Or ask the scholar to lend us his aid in comparing the best nations where Christianity was not, with the state to which it has brought us. Let him shew us countries literally depopulated by enervating vice and corruption; let him compare for us Christianity in its earliest growth with the filthy soil in which it grew; and we shall see how much cause there is to be thankful even on social grounds for the glorious gift of the Gospel. You that wish to take part in the ministry of Christ—to follow Him, and be His fishers of men—be sure that there is no place for misgiving as to the worthiness of your aim, as to the hopes you may form of doing good to your country and your kind. You glance back over the ages, and in spite of accidental differences, the conflict between good and evil has been in all ages the same. Ever has the call of God been listened to by His children, been treated with silent contempt by many, and by many been answered with malice and acrimony. It has ever brought peace and a sword; it has broken down the hard walls of some hearts by the very sound of its words, whilst others have resisted it unto death. But He that promised to be with us always to the end of the world, has been present with us by His Spirit as He promised. We know there is no change in Him who gives life to the Church, because the life has shewn no change. And your reward, if you labour for the Lord, will be the same in kind as that which sustained Paul, and John, and Peter when the world looked rugged all about them, and strove to frown them into inactivity. The child shall learn from you the way to God, and the evil passions it was born with shall be subdued. Taught by you, the bereaved family of some beloved father or mother shall learn not to sorrow as those without hope; the chastened grief of the Christian is far different from the wild funeral cries and gestures of the heathen's despair. You shall dig channels from the rich man's swollen purse to the poor man's barren dwelling, and the streams that flow down them shall bless both rich and poor alike. You shall tell the poor man of his dignity, as a soul beloved of Christ that bought him, and the suffering man of the elevation of mind he may reach through pains and troubles borne with resignation. Over your people and over you shall hover the perpetual shadow of God's presence; and you shall tell them that God is very near, as holy as He is clear-sighted, as just as He is holy. A great and glorious mission; only fruitless to that slothful servant that hides his Master's talent in the earth. To be messengers of God, ambassadors of Christ, sure that our message will be ratified by the Sender and accepted by the sent; to turn the people whom God loves from darkness to light, from the power of Satan unto God, and to present them to your Master on the day of account as those whom you have brought into His salvation,—earth has no better task for you!

Let me add, in conclusion, a few words of caution.

"Ye are the temple of the living God, as God hath said, I will dwell in them and walk in them; and I will be their God, and they shall be My people." Such is the mode of God's dealing with us. Our religion is not a book nor a Church, though it has both; it is an indwelling of God in the souls of His people, to sanctify them for Himself. Now as the miracles were given for an outward support of the Apostles' faith, so the works of the Spirit going on round us are the natural supports of ours. We have arrived at our own belief in the Gospel from the pious mothers, holy households, deeds of charity, able expounders of God's Word, that are scattered round us for a witness. And it is when we lose, or discard, or undervalue these supports, that critical enquiry becomes dangerous. It is not amongst the men that wrestle every day with evil in its practical shapes that misgivings spring up about the truth of the Gospel, but among men who within the four walls of their study look out upon the unmeasured ocean of possible doubts. And if any one who hears me now, feels strongly some of these doubts, I would not have him attempt to win through them by study alone. I would place him where Christian work was being done already, and ask him to make proof of his own power of well-doing. I would shew him that the Gospel was true for others by the evidence of their whole lives, and that in his own hands it is operative, potent, prevailing. Many a man has thus found peace instead of doubt, whose position was once full of peril. Had such a man, for example, with a spirit of doubt ever rising within him, and yet with a willingness to devote himself for duty's sake, gone forth as a missionary and endeavoured to preach, to those who knew nothing of God, the Gospel he fain would believe to be true, all his dangers would have been increased. No response at first from those he taught, no cheering sight of the effects of the Gospel, no atmosphere of Christian peace to brace him, nothing but one man uttering as in the wilderness the announcement of the kingdom of heaven, in a voice of uncertain sound, and the mocking echoes answering him in his spiritual solitude! Deprived of the natural supports of faith, he would have been unable perhaps to resist the first opponent he might meet with, and the brute stolidity of one who could only say "This cannot be," might overthrow his faith and turn him backward. One of our holiest missionaries, when first exposed to the keen air of Hindu unbelief, found himself obliged for his own sake to reconsider the evidences of Christianity from the beginning.

Read then the Bible and examine it. Cast upon it whatever light history or scholarship can throw. But do not forget that to understand the ways of God you must adore Him as a living power working ever in the world, whose footsteps are known by sin conquered and holiness established. We will not only read, we will adore the Lord who has hallowed our earth and made of our bodies His temple; who at the head of all that will fight for Him is carrying on the fight with Satan that has gone on for centuries, and will last till the sun of the world shall set for ever. In the ranks of that army we shall find support for our faith. And the light from heaven shines not more dimly in the nineteenth century than it shone in the first. We shall be near Him if we work with Him, if we conquer lusts and selfishness, if we love the truth and the right. God the Holy Spirit is ready to take possession of our minds. "To be spiritually minded is life and peace." "The God of hope fill you with all joy and peace in believing, that ye may abound in hope through the power of the Holy Ghost."

SERMON II.

The Spirit, a Divine Person, to be Worshipped and Glorified.

BY

H. L. MANSEL, B.D.,
WAYNFLETE PROFESSOR OF MORAL AND METAPHYSICAL PHILOSOPHY.

The Spirit, a Divine Person, to be Worshipped and Glorified.

GENESIS i. 2.

"And the earth was without form and void; and darkness was upon the face of the deep. And the Spirit of God moved upon the face of the waters."

ONE of the most remarkable features in the language of the Old Testament Scriptures is its power of *adaptation*, if we may so call it, which enables it in many instances to serve a twofold purpose in relation to those to whom it was first given, and to those who were to come after them. Principally, though not exclusively, is this character to be found in those portions of the earlier Revelation, which by way of prophecy, of type, and in some instances even of apparently mere narrative, were yet designed by the Holy Spirit through whose inspiration they were written, as an intimation and foreshadowing of Him that was to come, of Him of whom Moses and the Prophets wrote, unconsciously perhaps, or with but a partial consciousness of the full import of that which they were writing; but guided under a higher influence than their own to utter and record words whose full significance it was reserved for a later revelation to declare. How often do we find in Scripture that remarkable phenomenon of words bearing a double sense, looking partly to the present, but more fully to the future; having a meaning to convey and a purpose to serve towards those to whom they were first given, which yet was not their whole meaning; pointing onwards, faintly indeed and darkly, as must needs be the case till they are read by the light of their fulfilment, but yet certainly, to some further signification which in the fulness of time is seen to fit itself to them; bearing an interpretation, unsuspected it may be, until the event to which it points shall have appeared, yet nevertheless when that event has appeared, seen at once and manifestly to be a true interpretation. Some obvious examples of this, for instance, are furnished by those precepts and observances under the elder covenant which have a remote and typical as well as an immediate and literal significance. The Passover, to a devout Jew before the coming of Christ, had a meaning and a purpose, as a commemoration of the delivery of his people from the bondage of Egypt; but how much fuller and deeper significance does it acquire in our eyes, as pointing forward to the sacrifice of the true Passover, the Lamb without blemish and without spot, slain for the sins of the whole world. The ceremonies of the Day of Atonement conveyed to the Jewish worshipper their lesson concerning sin and its penalty and its expiation, of an offended and propitiated God; yet how much new light is thrown on the seemingly strange and obscure details of its observance by the Christian interpretation of their further import, "Christ being come an high priest of good things to come, by a greater and more perfect tabernacle, not made with hands, that is to say, not of this building; neither by the blood of goats and calves, but by His own blood He entered in once into the holy place, having obtained eternal redemption for us[a]." The brazen serpent, lifted up in the wilderness, had its immediate purpose in the healing of those who looked upon it; yet our Lord tells us of a further meaning fulfilled in Himself, "As Moses lifted up the serpent in the wilderness, even so must the Son of Man be lifted up, that whosoever believeth in Him should not perish, but have eternal life[b]." With the key to this method of Scripture furnished by such plain and striking examples as these, we may proceed with more confidence to the recognition of the same principle in other instances where the twofold application enters in a somewhat different manner; in the language of David for example, in the twenty-second and sixty-ninth Psalms, uttered in the first instance as a prayer called forth by his own sufferings, but moulded at the same time, under the influence of the Holy Spirit, to be a more exact prediction of the future sufferings of Christ: in the language of the same royal prophet, partially declaring in the first instance the establishment of his own kingdom,

[a] Heb. ix. 11, 12.　　　[b] St. John iii. 14, 15.

but finding a fuller and more complete application in relation to the spiritual kingdom of Christ[c]: in the language of Isaiah and Jeremiah, answering in some degree, and no doubt in earlier times understood as answering, to the temporal restoration of their country from captivity, but containing much also which can hardly have borne any clear and definite meaning till its further fulfilment in the spiritual restoration of mankind by Christ[d]. And finally, led on by the clear evidence of the existence of such a method in Scripture, we shall be able to accept with less hesitation those less obvious instances in which the primary sense of the passage appears at first sight to exhaust its entire significance, as it probably did exhaust all of which the sacred writer himself was conscious, as when the language of Hosea, having a natural reference to the past history of his nation—" When Israel was a child, then I loved him, and called my son out of Egypt[e]," is yet, by the use of the significant words "a child" and " my son," made to bear a further meaning in reference to an event corresponding by way of antitype in the life of the infant Saviour; or when the words of Jeremiah, referring directly to the captivity of Israel[f], yet, by being more directly associated with one portion of the captive tribes and one spot of the desolated country, the children of Rachel and her grave in

---

[c] *e.g.* Ps. ii., lxxxix., cxxxii.   [d] Isa. lii., Jer. xxxi.
[e] Hosea xi. 1; St. Matt. ii. 15.   [f] Jer. xxxi. 15; St. Matt. ii. 17, 18.

the road leading to Bethlehem, are made to bear a second relation, unknown till the event brought it to light, to the slaughter of the Innocents around the spot of our Lord's birth.

It is, perhaps, not altogether fanciful, if we seem to discern some traces of an analogy in this respect between the method of Scripture in dealing with those religious truths which it is directly designed to teach, and its method in relation to those natural truths which do not lie within its direct province, but which, nevertheless, incidentally and indirectly, it has at times occasion to take notice of. It may be that the language of Scripture, in relation to the phenomena of nature, is cast for the most part in a mould adapted to the knowledge and intelligence of the age in which it was written, and naturally so, as having an immediate significance in relation to that age: it may be that that language, interpreted by that knowledge alone, and without the aid of the light cast upon it by subsequent discoveries, would not of itself suggest the existence of another possible application beyond: it may be that the sacred writers themselves, in making use of language intelligible in their own day, were not distinctly conscious of any other import: it may be that their own positive knowledge in this respect was not greater than that of others of their age and nation;—still, when all this is admitted, there yet remain two remarkable facts to be taken into consideration; first, the fact of an expansiveness in the text of Scripture, whereby it is enabled in natural things to adapt itself to new discoveries of science, as we have seen that in spiritual things it adapts itself to new revelations of religious truth; and secondly, carrying the analogy into further detail, the fact that there are parts of the language of Scripture which, when interpreted only by contemporaneous knowledge, seem dark and unintelligible, or even altogether erroneous, but which acquire meaning and consistency, and even scientific accuracy, when viewed by the light of a later advancement of knowledge. A remarkable instance of the first of these facts will be found if we compare the Mosaic account of the creation of the world with any of the various cosmogonies of heathen poetry and mythology. In examining the various methods which have been adopted by Christian students of science in order to reconcile the Scriptural narrative of the creation with the results of modern discoveries, we may find, no doubt, interpretations of the language of Scripture which would not have suggested themselves as the most probable meaning of the words to the majority of men reading them before those discoveries were made (though some of these interpretations have even by such men been sometimes adopted as possible, prior to any apparent scientific necessity for their adoption): we may find also alternative hypotheses, suggesting different possible modes of reconciliation, between which, in our present state of knowledge, we are unable positively to decide which is entitled to the preference: we may find some difficulties not satisfactorily cleared up by any method as yet proposed, and perhaps awaiting the solution of a more advanced state of science and a more comprehensive survey of its conclusions than is at present possible: we may find all this, (and something very like this might have been found by a pious Jew, studying the types and prophecies of the Old Testament before the light that was shed upon them by the coming of Christ); but along with all this we also find, in the general tenor of the narrative, and to some extent even in its minuter details as well, a breadth, an expansiveness, a capacity of meeting new facts as they arise, which merely human imaginations and traditions wholly fail to exhibit. And when the defenders of the Bible, as an inspired record, are taunted, as they sometimes are by antagonists, with stretching the language of Scripture to meet the necessities of the case, let us ask ourselves, as we well may, what manner of book that must be which can stand the process and not give way under the tension. Try the same process on a heathen legend, it remains rigidly immoveable, or it breaks to pieces in your hands. Let us remember also that many an interpretation which has seemed strange and unnatural while it was new, has shewn itself natural and reasonable as it has become more familiar, as it has established itself as part of the accustomed current of men's thought and speech. Older sciences have had their day of supposed antagonism to Scripture, and Scripture to them, which now move quietly along with it side by side, neither harming and neither fearing the other. The time has been when the truth of Scripture was supposed to be in jeopardy from its alleged discrepancies with astronomical observations, and even with mathematical theorems; the same objections when revived by captious criticism now, are justly regarded as too contemptible to be worth a serious thought. The time may come, may even now be not far off, when the difficulties of our own day may meet with a similar fate, and, like all such difficulties when once fairly overcome, may but add to the strength of the fortress they were designed to overthrow.

The other characteristic of the language of Scripture, that advancing knowledge sometimes renders portions of it clearer and more intelligible which might once have seemed obscure or erroneous, is remarkably illustrated by one of the details of the same narrative. That God said "Let there be light, and there was light," before the formation of the apparent sources of light, the sun, the moon, and the stars, has constituted so much of a stumbling-block in the way of receiving the record as it stands, that unbelievers in earlier times have triumphed in bringing it forward as insurmountable; and moderns, who might have known better, have repeated the worn-out cry as a new discovery. Yet in point of fact this apparent anomaly is one not only allowed, but absolutely required, by one of the most plausible theories which modern science has proposed in explanation of the origin of our planetary system,—a theory invented with no reference to the Scripture narrative, yet harmonizing with it in this respect almost as closely as if it had been devised for the very purpose. Another illustration of the same kind is furnished by the wonderful coincidences between science and Scripture in the broad outlines of their several statements; in the harmony, too close to be the result of mere accident, as regards the general method and order of the creative work; and in the circumstance, that these agreements for the most part are found in unambiguous statements concerning matters of fact, while the apparent discrepancies for the most part turn upon questions of interpretation, such as that of the literal or figurative meaning of isolated words or sentences.

It may, therefore, be reasonably maintained that there is evidence of the existence of a method in Scripture, a method pursued alike in relation to those religious truths which it is its direct purpose to communicate, and to those natural truths which it touches upon only indirectly and in passing by, —a method, the characteristic feature of which is, that it refuses to anticipate that which is hereafter to be made known, whether by a fuller revelation in God's appointed time, or by the gradual progress of man's natural knowledge; and that, in consequence of this refusal, its earlier announcements are expressed in language partially imperfect and obscure, and admitting of various modes of supplement and explanation, until the time comes when the correlative facts are made known in their completeness, and the counterpart vindicates its own claim, by fitting into and harmonizing with all that has gone before.

The best example, perhaps, of this method will be seen by comparing the fulfilled prophecies relating to our Lord's first advent upon earth with the yet unfulfilled prophecies of His second advent;—the predictions of Isaiah, for instance, with those of St. John in the Apocalypse. How hard it would have been beforehand to construct an imaginary portrait of any one life and character, which should realise in all its details that marvellous combination of majesty and lowliness, of glory and humiliation, of power and suffering, which are shadowed forth in the prophetic description of the Messiah; yet how perfectly is every lineament realised, when we compare the whole with the Christ of the New Testament. How hard it is now, in spite of many remarkable coincidences which subsequent history has supplied, to conceive the exact course of events which shall fulfil in all its details the Apocalyptic vision; which yet doubtless, in its own time, will explain itself, as the Old Testament prophecies have done, by the light of its fulfilment. To believe this, is but to believe that that will be true concerning the method of Scripture in time to come, which has been true concerning the method of Scripture in time past.

We have seen this method of the Holy Spirit in Scripture exhibited in two of its applications,—as regards the visible world, and as regards the redemption of man and the person of the Redeemer. It remains that we examine it in relation to that which is more immediately the object of our present meditations. With the Spirit's witness concerning nature, and the Spirit's witness concerning Christ, we have to compare a third instance, the Spirit's witness concerning Himself.

Concerning the Person of the Divine Spirit, as concerning the Person of the Divine Son, we find intimations in the Old Testament, harmonizing with and naturally interpreted by the fuller revelation of the New; intimations which, without that fuller revelation, might be regarded rather as permitting than as necessitating such an interpretation; while with it they are seen to fall into their natural place in the order of a gradual and progressive manifestation of God to man, forming a part of a regular and connected whole, the work of one Divine Mind, "fitly joined together and compacted by that which every joint supplieth." In the opening words of Scripture, in the record of the creation of the world, we read that "the Spirit of God moved upon the face of the waters:" and that this language does not denote a mere poetic personification of a Divine Attribute, but refers—obscurely indeed, but naturally and properly—to a personal plurality in the Divine Nature, which in that plurality is yet One, is intimated by the words which follow shortly afterwards, "And God said, Let *us* make man in *our* image, after *our* likeness;" compared with the succeeding verse, "So God created man in *His* own image[g]." Such words, when read without the key which the Christian revelation supplies, would naturally seem strange and incongruous, and such as the natural knowledge of a mere human writer would hardly have suggested to him; but they acquire consistency and significance by the light that is shed upon them through the manifestation of God as a Trinity in Unity. Reading on a little way, we meet with another intimation of the nature and operation of the Divine Spirit: He is spoken of as striving against the wickedness of man: "And the Lord said, My Spirit shall not always strive with man[h];"—words which again acquire a new and fuller significance when supplemented by the language of our Lord, which tells us how the Comforter, when He is come, will reprove the world of sin, and that of St. Paul, contrasting the works of the flesh with the fruits of the Spirit, the one contrary to and lusting against the other[i]. In the later books of the Old Testament, the Spirit of God is represented with further indications of His work in relation to man. The Spirit of God speaks by the prophets. He is made known as the inspiring power through whom the long series of God's servants who delivered His commands to His chosen people were commissioned and qualified for their task. The Spirit is upon Moses and upon the elders appointed to assist him;

[g] Gen. i. 26, 27. [h] Gen. vi. 3.
[i] St. John xvi. 8; Gal. v. 17—23.

"and when the Spirit rested upon them, they prophesied, and did not cease[k]:" the Spirit that was in Elijah in like manner rests upon Elisha[l]: Ezekiel is brought in a vision by the Spirit of God into Chaldæa[m]: Zechariah testifies concerning "the words which the Lord of Hosts hath sent in His Spirit by the former prophets[n]." And not of the prophets only, but of Him to whom the prophets bare witness, is it testified beforehand that the Spirit of the Lord should be upon Him. Isaiah, speaking in the name of Christ, declares, "The Lord God and His Spirit hath sent me;" and again, "The Spirit of the Lord God is upon me;" and of Him, "The Spirit of the Lord shall rest upon Him[o]:" and the fulfilment of these predictions is shewn, when at His baptism the Spirit of God was seen descending like a dove and lighting upon Him, and confirmed by His own words when in the synagogue at Nazareth He opened the book of Isaiah and read the place where it was written, "The Spirit of the Lord is upon Me[p]." And finally, that same gift of the Holy Spirit which Isaiah announces in prophesying of Christ, is foretold by Joel in like manner concerning the servants of Christ: "And it shall come to pass afterward, that I will pour out My Spirit upon all flesh; and your sons and your daughters shall prophesy; your old men shall dream dreams, your young men shall see visions; and also upon the servants and upon the

---

[k] Numb. xi. 17, 25.   [l] 2 Kings ii. 15.   [m] Ezek. xi. 24.
[n] Zech. vii. 12.   [o] Isa. xlviii. 16; lxi. 1; xi. 2.   [p] St. Matt. iii. 16; St. Luke iv. 16—19.

handmaids in those days will I pour out My Spirit:" and the fulfilment of this prophecy is proclaimed by St. Peter on the day of Pentecost, when the cloven tongues as of fire sat upon the Apostles, and they were all filled with the Holy Ghost [q].

If we compare together the language of the Old and of the New Testament in relation to the Second and the Third Persons of the blessed Trinity, so far as the Divine Nature alone is spoken of, it is scarcely possible not to be struck with the exact analogy between the methods pursued in the revelation of each; it is scarcely possible not to see how each revelation, from a similar beginning, advances gradually but surely towards a similar conclusion. If the nature of the Divine Son is dimly indicated to the people of the older dispensation as the Angel of the Divine Presence, the Messenger of the Covenant, the Word of the Lord by whom the heavens were made [r],—expressions which, until interpreted by a later revelation, might be considered as permitting or at most suggesting, rather than as necessitating, the belief in a distinct Divine Person; the import of such language becomes no longer doubtful when it is viewed as an anticipation and foreshadowing of the more explicit declarations of the New Testament, converging to and summed up in the emphatic and unambiguous declaration of St. John, "In the beginning was the Word, and the Word was with God, and the Word

---

[q] Joel ii. 28, 29; Acts ii. 16—18.   [r] Exod. xxi.i. 20; xxxiii. 14; Isa. lxiii. 9; Mal. iii. 1; Ps. xxxiii. 6.

was God^s." And so too, if the language of the Old Testament concerning the Divine Spirit, taken alone and by itself, might leave some doubt on the minds of its readers whether it is to be understood as denoting a Divine Person or merely a divine influence, the doubt is for ever set at rest, and the right interpretation authoritatively fixed, by supplementary revelations in the New Testament, which admit of one meaning and one meaning only, "The Comforter, which is the Holy Ghost, whom the Father will send in My name, He shall teach you all things[t]:" "If I go not away, the Comforter will not come unto you; but if I depart, I will send Him unto you; and when He is come, He will reprove the world of sin, and of righteousness, and of judgment[u]:" "The Spirit helpeth our infirmities; ... the Spirit itself maketh intercession for us[x]:" "But all these worketh that one and the selfsame Spirit, dividing to every man severally as He will[y]." Words like these, summed up as they are and consecrated to the perpetual use of the Church by the parting injunction of her Lord,—that injunction which contains at once the confession of the Church's faith and the form of admission into her fold, "Go ye and teach all nations, baptizing them in the Name of the Father, and of the Son, and of the Holy Ghost[z],"—declare clearly and beyond all question what was the purport from the beginning of that continuous revelation, and the truth to

[s] St. John i. 1.   [t] Ibid. xiv. 26.   [u] Ibid. xvi. 7, 8.
[x] Rom. viii. 26.   [y] 1 Cor. xii. 11.   [z] St. Matt. xxviii. 19.

which it leads us—teach plainly and unambiguously the doctrine to which all Scripture bears witness—that of the Divine Personality, as of the Son, so also of the Holy Ghost.

Such is the method, and such the teaching, of the Divine revelation concerning the Holy Spirit. Gradually has its light advanced, brightening as it advances, from the first streak of dawn to the fulness of noon, from the first record of the creation of the world by Divine power to the last tidings of man's salvation by Divine love, telling us of one and the same Triune God, taking His threefold part in the first work and in the last. Round this culminating truth of the nature of the third Divine Person of the blessed Trinity gathers, as round its nucleus and centre, all that the same Scripture tells us of His dealings with us or of our duties towards Him. In that revelation of God the Holy Ghost we learn to know His blessed work in supplying the helplessness and strengthening the weakness of our fallen nature. He is manifested to us in His various offices of love and mercy, teaching, reproving, interceding, comforting, sanctifying. We learn, too, our duties towards Him, and those duties invested with additional solemnity and sanctity by the awful and mysterious doctrine of His presence in us. We learn not merely the special duties necessarily implied in our acknowledgment of Him as God, the duties of worship and obedience, of prayer and praise and giving of glory; but those moral obligations also, which the light of nature

make this prayer in sincerity; and to receive that renewing of the soul whereby alone we can walk worthily of our calling, through the operation of that blessed Spirit from whom the gift cometh; to whom, with the Father and the Son, three Persons and one God, be ascribed all honour and glory, world without end.

SERMON III.

The Spirit, the Teacher of the Church.

BY

CHR. WORDSWORTH, D.D.,
CANON OF WESTMINSTER.

The Spirit, the Teacher of the Church.

JOHN xiv. 26.

"The Comforter, which is the Holy Ghost, whom the Father will send in My Name, He shall teach you all things."

"IT is expedient for you that I go away," said our Blessed Lord to His disciples a little before His Passion, "for if I go not away, the Comforter will not come unto you; but if I depart, I will send Him unto you[a]." And the benefits which the Holy Ghost would confer upon them are expressed in these words; "When He, the Spirit of Truth, is come, He will guide you into all truth[b];" and again, "The Comforter, which is the Holy Ghost, whom the Father will send in My Name, He shall teach you all things[c]." And our Lord added the cheering assurance that the Holy Ghost, once given, would never depart from His Church: "I will pray the Father, and He shall give you another Comforter, that He may abide with you for ever; even the Spirit of Truth; whom the world cannot receive, because it seeth Him not, neither knoweth Him: but ye know Him; for He dwelleth with you, and shall be in you[d]." Thus, then, we see that Christ, who is the Truth, has promised

[a] John xvi. 7. [b] Ibid. 13. [c] Ibid. xiv. 26.
[d] Ibid. 16, 17.

that the Holy Ghost should *remain for ever* in His Church, *to teach her all things, and to guide her into all truth.*

The Holy Spirit's office of teaching and guidance is twofold. He performs it, first, by producing right *moral dispositions;* and secondly, by giving clear *spiritual perceptions.*

The former is His work of *sanctification;* the latter, that of *illumination;* and in order that we may be illuminated, we must first be sanctified.

Whatever the world may think, it is evident from Holy Scripture that *right moral dispositions* are an essential pre-requisite for *clear spiritual perceptions.* "The fear of the Lord is the beginning of wisdom[e];" and our Blessed Lord says, "If any man willeth to do God's will, he shall know of the doctrine[f]."

I. The *need* of the Holy Spirit's teaching and guidance is evident from our *natural* state. Our condition by *nature* is one of darkness and uncertainty, of proneness to evil and aversion from good. "God hath made man upright; but they have sought out many inventions[g];" "The natural man receiveth not the things of the Spirit of God: for they are foolishness unto him, because they are spiritually discerned[h]."

[e] Ps. cxi. 10; Prov. ix. 10.
[f] John vii. 17. Ἐάν τις θέλῃ τὸ θέλημα αὐτοῦ ποιεῖν γνώσεται περὶ τῆς διδαχῆς.
[g] Eccles. vii. 29.   [h] 1 Cor. ii. 14.

The world's history bears witness to this truth. The progress of *knowledge* is a very different thing from the increase of *wisdom*. Intellectual gifts often co-exist with much spiritual blindness. Remember the dark picture which St. Paul has drawn of the moral and spiritual condition of the most illustrious nations of antiquity; they were "filled with unrighteousness, fornication, wickedness; full of envy, deceit, malignity; despiteful, proud, boasters, disobedient to parents, without natural affection, implacable, unmerciful[i]."

He does not deny that they had many intellectual gifts, but he asserts that these gifts were even a snare to them, because they engendered pride. "The world by wisdom knew not God[j]." No; rather its "knowledge puffed it up[k];" "professing themselves wise, they became fools; they were vain in their imaginations, and their foolish heart was darkened[l];" they were "alienated from the life of God through the ignorance that was in them, because of the blindness of their heart[m]."

2. Not only was this the case with the world, but even with the Church herself as long as she was without the teaching and guidance of the Holy Ghost.

Although the Apostles enjoyed intimate communion with Christ during His ministry on earth, yet even at its close they were defective in right

---

[i] Rom. i. 29—31.   [j] 1 Cor. i. 21.   [k] Ibid. viii. 1.
[l] Rom. i. 21, 22.   [m] Eph. iv. 18.

moral dispositions and in clear spiritual perceptions. Even at the institution of the Holy Eucharist,—the Christian festival of love,—they "contended which of them should be the greatest[n];" even after His resurrection He had cause to *reprove them for their blindness and hardness of heart:*—"O fools, and slow of heart to believe all that the Prophets have spoken[o];" "He appeared to the eleven, and upbraided them with their unbelief and hardness of heart[p]." And even at the end of the forty days, just before His ascension, they were still very imperfectly schooled in the nature of His kingdom, and were ambitious of temporal sway:—"Lord, wilt Thou at this time restore again the kingdom to Israel[q]?" As yet the veil was on their hearts: and why? Because the Holy Ghost was not yet given.

3. But a new era was at hand. The promise of Christ was about to be fulfilled. "Ye shall receive power, after that the Holy Ghost is come upon you. Ye shall be baptized with the Holy Ghost not many days hence[r]."

The day of Pentecost arrived. Christ "was now gone up on high, and had led captivity captive, and had received gifts for men. He sent a gracious rain upon His inheritance, and refreshed it when it was weary[s]." The place in which the Apostles were assembled shook as with a mighty rushing wind, and the Holy Ghost descended on them "in tongues

---

[n] Luke xxii. 24.   [o] Ibid. xxiv. 25.   [p] Mark xvi. 14.
[q] Acts i. 6.   [r] Ibid. 8, 5; Luke xxiv. 49.   [s] Ps. lxviii. 9, 18.

of fire, which sate upon each of them." The wind and the earthquake shewed the might of the Spirit. The fire and the light were witnesses of His power in illumining the heart with the beams of heavenly wisdom, and in warming it with the holy flame of zeal and love. The streaming down of the tongues in a golden shower from heaven was a sign that He would endue them with divine eloquence; and the diffusion of the fiery tongues, and the burning of a heavenly flame on the head of each of them,— as if each was now consecrated to be an altar of the Holy Ghost,—was a token that the light of the Gospel, revealed from heaven, would rest upon them, and would burn brightly, and run like a living fire throughout all the world.

4. Let us remark the *effects* of the coming of the Holy Ghost.

The Apostles became new men. They, who a few days since had forsaken Christ and fled, now suffered gladly for Him. One of their number, who had quailed at a woman's voice in the high-priest's hall, and had thrice denied his Master, now valiantly confessed Him in the presence of priests and Pharisees, and charged them with having killed the Just One[t]. They who had taken refuge in an upper room with closed doors "for fear of the Jews," now came forward in streets and public places, and in the sight of all men "spake the word with boldness[u]." They who so lately had

[t] Acts iii. 14, 15, vii. 52.   [u] John xx. 19; Acts iv. 31.

striven together who should be the greatest, now "had all things common [v]." They whose eyes were blinded that they could not understand the Scriptures concerning their Master, had now a "mouth and wisdom which all their adversaries were not able to gainsay [w]," and now proved from those Scriptures that He is very Christ. They who had been dumb with dismay, and could scarcely speak their own language with propriety, (for the Galilæan dialect of St. Peter bewrayed him to be illiterate and of a despised province [x],) now spake with holy eloquence in every language under heaven, "as the Spirit gave them utterance [y]."

Such was the agency employed by God to teach the Apostles: such were the results of the coming and operation of the Holy Ghost.

5. Here, then, is our guide and example. The baptism of the Apostles with the Holy Ghost and fire from heaven declared that He is the Author of all virtuous practice and the Giver of all true wisdom. "The Comforter, which is the Holy Ghost, He shall teach you all things, He shall guide you into all truth."

Therefore let us boldly say that no system of teaching can produce the blessed fruits of truth, peace, and love, unless the Spirit of truth, and peace, and love, the Heavenly Dove, brood over it with His *silver wings, and His feathers like gold.*

---

[v] Acts ii. 44, iv. 32.   [w] Luke xxi. 15.
[x] Matt. xxvi. 73.   [y] Acts ii. 4.

No parent or teacher can teach aright, no scholar can learn aright, unless they are under the influence of the Holy Ghost. No parent or teacher can move the deeply-rooted mountains of pride, perverseness, frowardness, and wilfulness *in his own heart*, and in that of his children and scholars, except by the divine lever of prayer for the gifts and graces of the Comforter. Without His vivifying power we lie lifeless, like Lazarus, in a dark and noisome cave; we are wrapt and bound with grave-clothes; we are sealed up with a heavy stone on the tomb's mouth: and so we must remain for ever, unless the divine voice says to us, "Lazarus, come forth."

6. Let us not, however, be misunderstood.

We do not now expect to see the heavens opened, or to hear divine voices, or to feel our churches shaken with a mighty rushing wind, or to behold fire shooting from the clouds, or cloven tongues rained down upon us from the sky, or to see men suddenly rapt with divine ecstasies, and endued with gifts of prophecy, and speaking languages which they never learnt. No, these marvellous endowments *were* vouchsafed at the day of Pentecost, and in the first ages of the Church. They were given to prove the power and love of the Everlasting Spirit, and to shew us where our strength lies. But they were only for a time, and are now withdrawn,—not because the "Lord's arm is shortened," or because He does not now operate upon us, but because they have served their purpose, and done their duty of proving our need, and His might and mercy; and because He *now* gives *other, ordinary,* graces in their place, which are abundantly sufficient for the work of Christian teaching.

The Holy Ghost descended on the day of Pentecost in fulfilment of Christ's promise, and ever since that time, He—the Blessed Comforter—has been, is, and ever will be, with the Church. He will remain with her even to the end. And we are not now to look for His operations in the earthquake, or in the mighty wind, or in the fire, but in the still small voice of prayer, and in the gentle motions and whisperings of the Spirit in the hearing and reading of God's Holy Word; and in the silent hours of meditation, and in the calm effusions of grace, in the regular ministries of religion, in the house of God.

Let us not, however, imagine that these *ordinary* operations of the Holy Ghost, which are *now* vouchsafed to *us*, are less supernatural, because they are less audible and visible. No; they are as much beyond all human power and knowledge as was the descent of the fiery tongues on the day of Pentecost.

The silent, dove-like descent of the Holy Spirit, gliding down on inaudible and invisible wings into the soul of a sleeping infant at Holy Baptism; the yearnings of the heart of the adult before Baptism, and for Baptism,—like the stirrings of the unborn babe in its mother's womb,—the gentle fall of grace, like that of a spring shower, or soft drops of dew, on the heart, in the hours of pious contemplation,—these are gifts of the Holy Ghost. The illumination of the soul with the beams of divine radiance, shed upon it in the hearing or reading of God's Word, and enabling it to see " the wondrous things of His law ;" the kindling of devout affections and longing aspirations, of the pure flame of love, and of the fires of holy zeal,—these are gifts of the Holy Ghost. The stirring of the languid heart with fresh breezes from heaven ; the making of the tongue vocal with sacred eloquence in prayer and praise ; the opening of the spiritual eye to the sight of heavenly joys at the sound of holy music; the thrill which vibrates to the inmost soul at the laying-on of apostolic hands in the holy rite of Confirmation ; the forgetfulness of earth and the unfolding of heaven before the eyes in the participation of the Holy Eucharist ; the drinking-in of new life, like sap received by the branch from the True Vine, making it put forth fresh leaves and rich fruits, in dutiful obedience, in lively faith and fervent love, in humility, quietness, and gentleness, in resignation, patience, hope and joy, amid the sorrows and dreariness of this life ; the cheering of the drooping spirit in hours of grief and despondency,—all these are gifts of the Holy Ghost. And though they are vouchsafed every day, every hour, and every moment of the Church's existence, yet they are no less mysterious and supernatural than the opening of heaven and the descent of the Spirit on the heads of the Apostles on the day of Pentecost; and they are some of the modes in which the Holy Ghost now exercises His divine office of teaching the world, and performs the work of moral sanctification, and fulfils our Lord's promise,—" The Comforter, which is the Holy Ghost, He shall teach you all things."

Let us now proceed to consider what was the charge which Christ gave to the Apostles, with a view to the teaching of mankind, when they themselves should have been taught by the Holy Ghost.

When Christ founded His apostolic school for the world, He said to them, "Go ye, teach all nations, baptizing them in the name of the Father, and of the Son, and of the Holy Ghost[y]." This was His royal charter of incorporation. The baptismal covenant is the germ of the world's education; and baptismal grace is the early rain which makes the tender shoot put forth its first leaves, which are afterwards to be watered with the fresh dews and latter rain of the Spirit, in prayer, and in the reading of God's Word, and in the gift of the Holy Spirit in Confirmation, and in the Holy Eucharist, and in the other regular ministrations of religion.

It has pleased God of His goodness to us to convey grace to our souls by these channels. And although He *could*, if He so willed it, give us grace by any *other* means than these, or *without* any means

[y] Matt. xxviii. 18, 19.

at all, yet since He has instituted these means for the purpose of conveying grace to us, *we* have no warrant to expect grace, unless we use—use diligently, thankfully, and devoutly—those means which He has appointed for that purpose, with express command to us to employ the same.

Hence the apostolic school of Christianity is thus described by the Holy Ghost: "They that were baptized continued stedfastly in the Apostles' doctrine and fellowship, and in breaking of bread, (that is, in participation in the Holy Eucharist,) and in prayers[z]."

II. Let us now apply these principles to our own practice.

1. In reviewing the history of mankind, and the provision made for its education by Christ Himself, we arrive at this conclusion, that no system of teaching (that is, of training for eternity) can do its proper work except it lay its foundation in a recognition of man's fall, and consequent weakness, blindness, and corruption, with regard to his best and highest interests.

2. Next, since "the preparations of the heart are from the Lord[a]," every sound system of teaching will proceed to acknowledge the necessity of Divine influence to purify the corruption, lighten the darkness, and assist the weakness of human nature.

3. Next, it will confess, and act habitually on

[z] Acts ii. 41, 42.   [a] Prov. xvi. 1.

the conviction, that this work of sanctification, illumination, and assistance, can only be performed by the HOLY GHOST. Let us, therefore, never imagine, that even instruction in Scripture itself will be profitable, without the spiritual help of Him by whose inspiration Scripture was written.

4. Next, since the grace of the Holy Spirit is given through regular channels, every right system of teaching will look to receive grace by those means; and will not expect grace unless it avail itself of them.

Let us, therefore, never concur with any who would divorce instruction from the public offices of religion. Schools and Colleges without prayer and Sacraments are "wells without water; clouds and wind without rain [b]." They are without the teaching of the Holy Spirit, the author of peace and love, who alone can "teach us all things and guide us into all truth."

5. Next, since Christ has instituted His Church to be the temple of the Holy Ghost, every sound system of teaching will look for grace, and truth, and peace where Christ gives it, and where it is sure of finding it. It will act on the persuasion that it cannot hope to teach aright except in communion with the Church of Christ.

III. Consider now the office of the Holy Ghost in teaching *spiritual truth*. The Holy Spirit was promised and given in order to *abide for ever* in the

[b] 2 Pet. ii. 17; Jude 12; Prov. xxv. 14.

Church, which is to extend to *all place*, and to subsist for *all time;* and the promise of our Lord was that the Holy Ghost would teach *her all things*, and guide her into *all truth;* that is, would teach her *all things* that are necessary for her spiritual mission to the world, and guide her into *all truth*, that is, into all *spiritual truth* that is requisite for our growth in grace here, and for our attainment of glory hereafter.

1. The question then is, *In what manner* has this divine promise been fulfilled? *How* does the Holy Spirit perform His office in the Church, of teaching all spiritual truth?

2. He has performed it in part by delivering to the Church the Holy Scriptures, which He has "written for our learning[c]," and which are "able to make us wise unto salvation through faith which is in Christ Jesus; and which are profitable for doctrine, for reproof, for correction, for instruction in righteousness, that the man of God may be perfect, throughly furnished unto all good works[d]." And He continues to perform it by guarding Holy Scripture and diffusing it by the agency of the Church, and by assuring us of the *inspiration* of Holy Scripture by her instrumentality; and also by giving us, by her means, the true *interpretation* of *Holy Scripture*.

What, let us ask, is the principal cause of doubt and disbelief with regard to the truth and inspiration of Scripture? It is this: men have forgotten the

[c] Rom. xv. 4.   [d] 2 Tim. iii. 15—17.

office of God the Holy Ghost, as the Guide and Teacher of the Church. They take up the Bible as "a common book," and criticise it as they would some Egyptian papyrus, or some ancient roll disinterred from the ashes of Pompeii or Herculaneum. They seem to forget, that as soon as the five Books of Moses were written, Almighty God provided an *external* witness, to assure men of their truth and inspiration. He separated those Books visibly and publicly from *all other* writings, by enshrining them in the *Holy of Holies* in the Tabernacle, and by placing them under the wings of the cherubim[e]. They appear to forget, that there never has been a Bible without a visible Church to guard and authenticate it, and to assure the world of its truth and inspiration. They separate the Message from the Messenger; they take away the Light from the Candlestick in which God's hand has placed it; they separate the Bible from the Church, and so they grieve the Holy Ghost, who speaks in the Bible and dwells in the Church; and they lose both the Bible and the Church. They overlook the all-important fact, that when the Son of God Himself came down from Heaven, and was "anointed with the Holy Ghost[f]," He set His own divine seal on the Old Testament, and avouched it to be true, genuine, and divine. They seem also to forget the no less momentous fact, that when the Son of God had ascended into heaven, and had given the Holy Ghost to His Church for the express purpose of "teach-

[e] Deut. xxxi. 9, 24—26; Josh. xxiv. 26. [f] Acts x. 38.

ing her all things," and of "guiding her into all truth," the Holy Ghost Himself gave His own divine testimony in the Church by the lips of the holy Apostles, to the truth, genuineness, and inspiration of the Old Testament; and that He has declared that "all Scripture is given by the inspiration of God[g]," and that "no prophecy of Scripture is of private interpretation; for prophecy came not in old time by the will of man: but holy men of God spake as they were moved by the Holy Ghost[h]." They seem also to overlook the fact, that the *New* Testament has been delivered to the Church by Apostles and Evangelists, who were taught, guided, and inspired by God the Holy Ghost, and that it was delivered by them for the express purpose of being read publicly in the Church; yes, of being read as of equal dignity with the *Old* Testament, which the Son of God Himself had acknowledged to be divine; and that the New Testament has been so received and read by the Church Universal, to which Christ promised that He would send the Holy Ghost to "teach her all things, and to guide her into all truth." And therefore this *reception* of the New Testament by the Church is no other than the witness of God the Holy Ghost to its truth and inspiration.

3. Thus, then, we see an uniform divine plan from the time in which the first letter of Scripture was written, even down to our own days, for avouching the truth and inspiration of the Bible. The

[g] 2 Tim. iii. 16.   [h] 2 Pet. i. 20, 21.

Pentateuch was placed in the Holy of Holies in the Tabernacle, and under the wings of the cherubim, and thus its inspiration was proclaimed by God to the world; and *both* Testaments are now placed under the wings of the Holy Ghost, the Divine Dove who descended on Christ at His baptism; they are safe under His feathers, in the tabernacle of the Christian Church.

4. If these truths are forgotten, as, alas! they too often are in these our days, which proudly boast their intellectual light but are clouded over with spiritual darkness, is it wonderful that men should disparage Scripture, and carp and cavil at it? No; these cavillings of theirs are the consequences of that spiritual blindness, which is their *punishment* for despising the witness of God the Holy Ghost. They will not listen to His teaching in the Church; they will not follow His guidance, and so they grieve the Holy Ghost, and provoke Him to leave them to themselves. And how *can* they see without Him who is the light? It is impossible. Impunity in sin is the worst punishment, and unconsciousness of blindness is the worst blindness. So awful is the punishment which they endure for despising the light of the Holy Ghost, that they presumptuously imagine that they themselves alone can see, and disdainfully despise others as blind, who are walking meekly and humbly " in the path of the just, which shineth more and more unto the perfect day[1]."

[1] Prov. iv. 18.

5. It is manifestly the intention of God that young children in our village schools and aged peasants in our cottages should believe that (as St. Paul affirms) " all Scripture is given by inspiration of God;" and it is also God's will that they should be able to give a *reason* for this belief, as St. Peter commands them to do :—" Be ready always to give an answer to every man that asketh you a reason of the hope that is in you¹."

But can it be imagined that children and peasants should examine all the objections that have been brought, or may be brought, against the inspiration of Scripture, or that they should postpone their belief in it till all those objections are examined by others ? Assuredly not. If this were the case they would be condemned to live without love, and to die without hope. What then shall they do ? They will humbly and reverently listen to the teaching of God the Holy Ghost dwelling in the Church, and testifying to the inspiration of the Bible. Here they are safe. The Bible is sheltered by the wings of the Holy Ghost dwelling in the Church. And if a child in our village schools or a peasant in our cottages is asked *why* he believes the Bible to be inspired, he may boldly give this answer,—' I believe the Bible to be inspired, because I believe in the Holy Catholic Church, and because I believe in God the Holy Ghost, and because I believe that God the Holy Ghost came down from heaven according to Christ's most true promise,

---

¹ 1 Pet. iii. 15.

to teach the Church *all things*, and to guide *her into all truth;* and I therefore receive the testimony of the Church Catholic to the inspiration of Holy Scripture, as no other than the testimony of God.'

And this is the ground on which the belief in the inspiration of Holy Scripture is placed by the Church of England in her Sixth Article:—" In the name of *Holy Scripture*" (i.e. of divinely-inspired writings, for the word γραφὴ, or *Scripture*, is not applied in the New Testament to *any other* writings) " we do understand those canonical Books of the Old and New Testament, of whose authority was never any doubt in *the Church*. . . . All the Books of the New Testament, as they are *commonly received*, we do receive, and account them canonical." Of course the Church of England does not exclude the other *internal* evidences of inspiration, in the Books themselves, and in the heart of the believer, who has the witness of the Spirit within him; nor does she forget the *external* evidences of inspiration, from fulfilment of prophecy, and from the good effects produced by the Scriptures: but *the* main ground on which she insists is the testimony of God the Holy Ghost in the Church Catholic, *receiving all* Holy Scripture as divine.

6. Once more. To believe in the inspiration of the Bible, is to believe the testimony of God; but it is *not enough* to believe in the inspiration of the Bible, we must also have the *true interpretation*

of the Bible. The *true sense* of the Bible *is* the Bible; a wrong interpretation of the Bible is not the Bible, but a corruption of it; it is a substitution of the word of *man* in the place of the Word of *God*.

It is plainly requisite, therefore, and it is manifestly God's design, that children in our schools and peasants in our cottages should have the *right interpretation* of the Bible in all things necessary for their salvation. Can we, then, imagine that God intended that they should be left to gather the doctrines of the Christian faith out of the Bible for themselves, or that they should be the victims of discordant sects and rival teachers, each claiming to have the true sense of the Bible? Assuredly not. What, then, is the true state of the case? Almighty God has not only given us a Bible, but He has also instituted and appointed a Church to declare to us its meaning; and accordingly the Church is described in Holy Scripture as the "Body of Christ[k]," "the pillar and ground of the truth[l]." He has sent the Holy Ghost from heaven to "lead her into all truth," to "teach her all things,"—especially the true meaning of the Bible. The Holy Ghost enabled the Apostles to *interpret* the types and prophecies of the Old Testament. And if men had duly considered this office of God the Holy Ghost in interpreting the Old Testament in the New, is it possible that we should have ever heard, what alas! we have lived to hear, the miserable cavils

[k] Col. i. 18, 24.   [l] 1 Tim. iii. 15.

of shortsighted men against the interpretations which He has given us of those prophecies, when He declares their true sense in the earlier chapters of the Gospel of St. Matthew, or in the sermons of St. Peter and St. Paul in the Acts of the Apostles?

And as to Christian *doctrine*, is it credible that we should have such unhappy bickerings as prevail among us concerning the meaning of Scripture with regard to the main articles of the faith, and such strainings and wrestings of single texts of Scripture in contravention of the drift and tenor of the whole, if we had duly remembered Christ's promise to His Church to send the Holy Ghost to "teach her all things, and lead her into all truth, and to abide with her for ever," and if we had duly revered that teaching as embodied in the common consent of the Catholic Church, especially in her Creeds and Confessions of Faith [m]?

[m] See Richard Baxter's Introduction to Catholic Theology, 1675. Baxter, who will not be charged with overrating the authority of the Church in Creeds and Confessions of Faith, thus writes:—"The Baptismal Covenant expounded in the ancient Creed, is the sum and symbol of Christianity. . . . Though I am not of their mind, that think the twelve Apostles each one made an Article of the Creed, or that they formed and tied men to just the very same syllables and every word that is now in the Creed; yet that they still kept to the same *sense* and *words*, *so* expressing it, as by their variation might not endanger the corrupting of the faith by a new sense, is certain from the nature of the case, and from the *agreement of all the ancient Creeds* which were ever professed at baptism from their days; that cited by me (Appendix to "Reformed Pastor") out of *Irenæus*, two out of *Tertullian*, that of *Marcellus* in *Epiphanius*, that expounded by *Cyril*, that in *Ruffinus*, the *Nicene Creed*, and all mentioned by Ussher and Vossius, agreeing thus far in

Surely it is a providential circumstance that the Church of Rome, amid her manifold errors and corruptions, has never ventured to use, in administering the Sacrament of Baptism, any other Creed besides the *Apostles' Creed;* and that in the celebration of the Sacrament of the Lord's Supper she has never dared to add her own Trent innovations to the ancient *Nicene* or *Constantinopolitan* Creed. And even the very vehemence with which the Eastern Church has debated with the Western on *one* minor article (concerning the procession of the Holy Ghost) of that Creed serves to bring out more strongly and clearly the *consent* of East and West in that Creed.

Here, then, we have Christ's promise fulfilled; here we have the teaching and guidance of the Holy Ghost in the Church. To this teaching and guidance our children and peasants may resort. Here they may find shelter. "Thou shalt hide them privily by Thine own presence, O Lord, from the provoking of all men: Thou shalt keep them secretly in Thy tabernacle from the strife of tongues [n]."

7. Finally, let me remind you, my younger brethren, that no intellectual gifts alone, however brilliant, will qualify you to discover or to receive divine

---

sense. And no one was baptized without the Creed professed. *As Christ Himself* was the *author of the Baptismal Creed and Covenant,* so the Apostles were the authors of that *exposition* which they then used and taught the Church to use. And they did *that* by the *Holy Ghost,* as much as their inditing of *Scripture."*

[n] Ps. xxxi. 22.

truths. You must have *moral dispositions* for the perception of *spiritual verities.* The Holy Spirit, as His Name declares, is a Spirit of purity, and no one is able to understand the teaching of the Spirit unless he leads a holy life. "The wisdom from above," says St. James, "is first pure, then peaceable[o]." "Blessed are the pure in heart: for they shall see God[p]." "Flee therefore youthful lusts[q];" they cloud and dim the spiritual eye; and remember that your bodies are "temples of the Holy Ghost which is in you[r]." Consecrate them to His service, and then you will be like the beloved disciple St. John, who leaned on Christ's bosom at supper, and drank heavenly wisdom from His mouth.

Remember also that the Holy Spirit is a *dutiful* Spirit, and will not dwell with the proud and vainglorious "disputer of this world," who sets up his own reason as a judge of divine revelation; but that He loves to abide with the humble-minded and meek-hearted. "I thank Thee, O Father," said Christ, "that Thou hast hid these things from the wise and prudent, and revealed them unto babes[s]." Heaven forbid that we should check enquiry. No: "Prove all things: hold fast that which is good[t]." But remember the precept of the Apostle, which precedes that which has been just cited. Before saying "Prove all things," he says "Quench not the Spirit[u]." And why? because it is vain to attempt

[o] James iii. 17.   [p] Matt. v. 8.   [q] 2 Tim. ii. 22.
[r] 1 Cor. vi. 19.   [s] Matt. xi. 25.   [t] 1 Thess. v. 21.
[u] Ibid. 19.

to *prove any thing* that is spiritual if we quench the Spirit who enables us to prove it. It is futile to enquire without the light of the Spirit, which is quenched by pride and self-conceit. Enquire; yes, but enquire with reverence and meekness, and with a humble sense of your own weakness and short-sightedness, and, most of all, your perpetual need of the help and illumination of God the Holy Ghost. " Mysteries are revealed unto the meek [x]." " Them that are meek shall He guide in judgment: and such as are gentle, them shall He learn His way [y]." We must " become as little children, if we would enter the kingdom of God [z]."

Next, also, the Holy Spirit is a Spirit of *fairness, honesty*, and *truth*. He abhors all disingenuousness and equivocation. They who tamper with their own consciences are *morally disqualified* for the discovery or reception of *spiritual truth*. The fact is, and it must be spoken, (for the unhappy circumstances of our own days require it,) any person who is admitted to any office in the Church, on making certain sacred engagements, and who, after he has been admitted thereto on the strength of those engagements, uses his office as a vantage-ground for attacking the truths which he has solemnly pledged himself to maintain, is guilty of grieving and provoking God the Holy Ghost; and it would therefore be a marvellous thing if he could discover or receive divine truth. His very objections against the truth of Holy Scripture, his cavils against its

[x] Ecclus. iii. 19.   [y] Ps. xxv. 8.   [z] Matt. xviii. 3.

inspiration, are precisely what might be expected under the circumstances of the case; they are the recoil of his own sin on himself for resisting the Holy Ghost. The Holy Ghost punishes him with blindness, because he turns away his face from the true light; He punishes him by allowing him to imagine that he can see, and even to boast of his own illumination, when all the while he is immersed in spiritual darkness.

"When I was young," says St. Augustine, "I studied the Bible with shrewdness of disputing, and not with meekness of enquiring, and thus I shut the door of Scripture against myself with my own hand[a]." "In order to understand Scripture, the first requisite is the fear of God. This fear of God makes us meditate upon death and judgment to come, and to bewail our own sins, and to nail our proud thoughts to the cross of Christ, and to bow down in lowly adoration before the majesty of Scripture; and to love God and man, and to cherish that purity to which the light of God's countenance is vouchsafed, and the truth in His Holy Word is revealed. The man who fears God seeks to learn God's will there. Such a man loves not strife, but is gentle and devout. He has skill in languages for the exposition of Holy Scripture; and he has the true text of Scripture derived from correct manuscripts. Thus furnished, he comes to its interpretation; and wherever he is in doubt he consults the Rule of faith, which is formed from the

[a] St. Aug. Serm. li.

plain places of Scripture, and from the authority of Christ's Church[b]."

Let us, therefore, seek the truth, not in proud disputations, but on our knees; in private prayer in our secret chamber, in public prayer in the Church of God; in the breaking of bread where Christ "is made known to us[c];" in the teaching of God the Holy Ghost, speaking to us in Christ's Church, to which He has promised His presence for ever:—"Lo, I am with you alway, even unto the end of the world[d]."

[b] St. Aug. De Doct. Christian., ii. 9, iii. 1, 2.
[c] Luke xxiv. 35.
[d] Matt. xxviii. 20.

SERMON IV.

The Spirit, the Giver of Life.

BY

T. L. CLAUGHTON, M.A.,
VICAR OF KIDDERMINSTER.

The Spirit, the Giver of Life.

GENESIS i. 2.

"And the Spirit of God moved upon the face of the waters."

AT the time concerning which these words were written, the whole substance or matter of which all things were to be created lay buried in water, a dark and shapeless void, of commingled and confused elements — primæval chaos. Who could infuse life into this mass? Who could produce order out of such confusion? beauty and harmony of parts, where no one thing either resembled, or was different or discrete from another? None but God.

We read accordingly that "the Spirit of God moved upon the face of the waters." The word "moved" here is a comprehensive word, containing both the idea of motion and of rest; it is the word by which we should describe the motion of the eagle fluttering over her nest, or the brooding of the hen over her young. And it is here used to signify the accession and effectual presence of an all-pervading Power, in which was life or breath, warmth, light, order, shape, and comeliness, to be communicated in successive developments to the dark waters which lay still and dead till this Influence passed upon them. "Thou sendest forth Thy Spirit; they are created: and Thou renewest the face of the earth," says the sweet Psalmist of Israel—summing up in those few words the history both of the original creation and of the continuance of life in every part of it; fathoming the depth of Moses' words, and ascribing unto that very Power whose operation is described to us in the words of the text the whole development of life in the material world, as it is seen to this day. The Holy Ghost moves: He is the first author and beginner, as He also establishes and perpetuates all life. We see in Him how the world began; how it still subsists; yea, and shall subsist, remodelled, restored, and renewed, for ever. He moves upon the face of the waters, and they, and all that lay beneath them, become by virtue of that operation instinct with life, or the seminal principle of life; capable of producing those creatures which they afterwards brought forth, in their various kinds and specialities.

Now we cannot doubt that He who was so wonderful in counsel and excellent in working—forecasting, as an artificer does, the form and effect and beauty of that which He designed—was not as some have imagined a mere power of God, but Very God Himself; which, though the Jews saw not, we in explicit teachings of the New Testament, which the Jews will not allow, recognise and adore. And yet they might have seen and understood if they had considered, and there were those among them all along who did consider—who saw the Lord of Life in His works of providence and in the gracious deliverances which He wrought for His people. Did not one of their own prophets bless and praise Him in the song " as clothed with majesty and honour; as crowning Himself with light as with a garment, and spreading out the heavens like a curtain; laying the beams of His chambers in the waters, and making the clouds His chariot, and walking upon the wings of the wind:" but much more than this, as prescribing limits to the waters, that they should no more overflow the earth, but go down into the valleys, and run among the hills, to refresh man and beast; as giving food to all flesh, to every kind that sort of food which is adapted to sustain life, the green herb for the cattle, and wine and bread for man; as appointing the moon to regulate the seasons, the rising and setting of the sun for labour and for rest; as opening His hand and filling all things with good; and (which is the matter we are especially considering) as giving, or by His departure taking away life at His will? Surely all this is consistent only with the idea of the Personal Godhead of Him whose moving on the face of the waters, as the first recorded act of creation, was in the mind and memory of all the children of Abraham. They were familiar, moreover, with the Book of Job, wherein the whole course of nature, as we call it, is ascribed to the working and the counsel of God, from the day when the foundations of the earth were fastened, and the sea shut up with doors, and the light divided from the darkness, down to the present personal experience and observation of them that were living upon the earth. Nor was the language of the Books with which they were so well acquainted less explicit as touching that influence of the Divine Spirit on the hearts and on all the ways of men, which established Him in their minds as the Lord and Giver of spiritual as well as natural life. To Him David prayed, "Thou art my God: Thy Spirit is good; lead me into the land of uprightness." And of Him spake Elihu, "The Spirit of God made me, and the breath of the Almighty gave me life[a]." Again, if Elihu complained that men were slow to acknowledge that they owed to the Creator Spirit the wisdom, and the speech, and other natural gifts they enjoyed above the rest of the creation: "None saith, Where is God my Maker, who giveth songs in the night; who teacheth us more than the beasts of the earth, and maketh us wiser than the fowls of heaven[b]?"—so did David ascribe to Him (for of whom else could he speak?) the purification of the inward parts, the knowledge of wisdom in the hidden part, i.e. of true spiritual wisdom, which is the life of the soul, for the soul that hath it not does not live, but is dead; without spiritual light is no life. It is the consciousness

---

[a] Job xxxiii. 4.   [b] Ib. xxxv. 10, 11.

of God's presence by which men live, and in which the life of the Spirit truly consists. This was the life which Hezekiah craved in his recovery from sickness, not the prolongation of his bodily life only: "they that go down to the pit," he said, "cannot hope for Thy truth." The thing he longed for was life wherewith to celebrate the praises of the Lord. And whence did he hope for the gift but from the Spirit of Life?

And in all this they ascribed a personal agency to the Lord the Spirit. That our sin is an offence against Him, our righteousness no gain to Him, is taught as plainly by the words of Elihu as by those of St. Paul. "If thou sinnest, what doest thou against Him? or if thy transgressions be multiplied, what doest thou unto Him? If thou be righteous, what givest thou Him? or what receiveth He of thine hand[c]?" His presence was acknowledged in the journeyings of the people; He was the Strength of Joshua, the Leader of the host of the Lord. He came on Balaam, on Othniel, Gideon, Jephthah, Samson, on Saul, on Azariah the son of Oded in King Asa's time. Zedekiah the son of Chenaniah, in his insulting question to Michaiah, recognised the Spirit of the Lord acting on the mind of the prophets. Micah was full of power by the Spirit of the Lord. Ezekiel, on God's business, was taken up by the Spirit and brought in a vision by the Spirit of God into Chaldea, to them of the

---

[c] Job xxxv. 6, 7.

captivity. Yea, of Him was the calling of the prophets, the anointing of the Son of God.

But there was a time to come when these things should be yet more plainly revealed and more fully understood, i.e. in such part of them as was yet dark and uncertain, albeit profitable,—yea, needful unto salvation,—for men to understand aright. In regard of the works of nature, and the creation of nature with that power to work, by the Spirit of God, the Jews saw as deep as we see into the Divine mysteries; they felt, as deeply as we feel them, the blessed and holy influences of this glorious and beautiful creation. Nor could they be far behind us in imputing all providential agencies in the world to Him who first moved in its creation. But they knew not yet how the mystery of the waters bringing forth the world by the power of the Spirit, contained under it another and a deeper mystery, viz. how the Church of God should be born by the same means—how life should come again by water and the Holy Ghost. Nor had even those who lived toward the close of that dispensation gathered yet what we have gathered, by the teaching of the Lord Himself, from the salvation of Noah and his family in the ark from perishing by water, nor from the passage of the Israelites through the Red Sea, nor from the rock which Moses smote, no, nor from the words of the Prophet, "I will pour water on him that is thirsty, and floods upon the dry ground: I will pour My Spirit upon thy seed: and My blessing upon thine offspring: and they shall spring up as among the grass, as willows by the water courses;" so abundant shall be the gifts that I shall give them: —they could not, I say, fully understand these things: for why? The Holy Ghost was not yet given—given as a Gift; the way into the holiest of all was not yet manifest. The true ministration of the Spirit, the ministration of righteousness, the free gift which came upon all men unto justification of life was not yet established, because the first tabernacle was still standing. Jesus was not yet glorified. Men had yet to learn what the abundance of grace and the gift of life was, concerning which Jesus Christ spake those truly marvellous words, "He that believeth on Me, as the Scripture hath said, out of his belly shall flow rivers of living water." But at length the fulness of time was at hand, when the Lord, the Giver of life, should indeed dwell among His people, when God should pour out His Spirit upon all flesh.

He came with such gentleness as of itself betokened the nature of His work. He came, as He came at the first, moving on the water; yea, we believe He wrought on the waters in the creation because He designed to do so in the regeneration of man. He consecrated water to be the instrument of life. The record of this second spiritual creation is as grand as it is simple: "Now when all the people,"—all, that is, on a certain day, who had laid John the Baptist's words to heart,—" when all the people were baptized, it came to pass that Jesus also being baptized and praying, the heaven was opened, and the Holy Ghost descended in a bodily shape like a dove upon Him." Not that He had need of baptism unto life, or illumination, or any gift, who was the Light and Life Himself, and in whom all the fulness of the Godhead dwelt; but that in passing through the water for us He made it the instrument of our regeneration, and so fulfilled all righteousness; and established, beyond all doubt, the ark of Noah and the passage of the Red Sea to be types and figures of Baptism unto life. I say beyond all doubt, in the face of much doubt and questioning, — of words that eat like a canker; but whose words? The words, alas! of those who, by their own admission, enquire at the living oracles to find excuses for unbelief, and in hope that the weakness of the answer may justify them in at least partial unbelief; whom God therefore, as He is wont, answereth according to the idol they have set up in their heart; causing the shadow in which they walk, disquieting themselves in vain, to rest upon their unhallowed manner of dealing with His Word. And so it will rest till they shall be brought to search the Word in another spirit, as some have been brought already who had gone far astray, as more will be brought; though it can scarcely be supposed but that the influences of this present time will lead more—many more—astray, and these seeds of doubt, sown broadcast, will increase yet unto more ungodliness, and overthrow the faith of many. But let no man think that the Spirit of life can become the Spirit of death, as these would make Him to be; and that He whom the Saviour Himself foretold should come as the Spirit of Truth to guide His people into all truth, should mislead —should have misled through so many ages—the best and holiest of mankind.

It were impossible—absolutely impossible—that the Church of the living God, the pillar and ground of the truth, should have been proclaiming a lie throughout all these ages; should be a savour of death to those who sought to her for life; a shroud of darkness to the baptized, the illuminated, the chosen and beloved of God. Let no man doubt that the great salvation prefigured by the saving of Noah and his family in the ark from perishing by water, and by the baptism of Israel in the cloud and in the sea, is secured to us and to our children by an ordinance for ever; and that all we who have been baptized into the death of Christ, shall, if we die with Him unto sin by continual mortification of our corrupt affections, have our part likewise in His glorious resurrection. Be it our comfort to know that in Holy Baptism the three witnesses coincide, the Spirit, the Water, and the Blood: the Blood there signifying our sin, that could only be expiated by blood; the Water our burial, through which we must pass unto our resurrection; and the Spirit imparting unto that body, dead through sin, the gift of life,—as it is written, "If Christ be in us, the body is dead because of sin; but the spirit is life because of righteousness."

But there is a yet further mystery of lifegiving by the Holy Spirit, which St. Paul goes on from the words just now quoted to declare, which is this: "If the Spirit of Him that raised up Jesus from the dead dwell in you, He that raised up Christ from the dead shall also quicken your mortal bodies by His Spirit that dwelleth in you." So that the goodness and mercy of God which have followed a true Christian all the days of his life, ever since the day when having been baptized into Christ he put on Christ, will not fail him even in the hour of dissolution, and when the last enemy shall come upon him. For his body being made a temple of the Holy Ghost, who is the Lord of Life, shall by the power of the Spirit of Life be quickened into life eternal. The blessing he has received by the power of the indwelling Spirit now, shall be as nothing to that which is in store for him when at the resurrection the Spirit of Life will enter again into the earthly tabernacle, and change it by His marvellous power from a corruptible to an incorruptible body. Then shall He enlighten our eyes, and enlarge our capacity, to behold the glory and majesty of God Himself: in the which hope David surmounted all his trouble; prophesying indeed of Christ when he said "My flesh shall rest in hope; for Thou wilt not leave my soul in hell, neither wilt Thou suffer Thine Holy One to see corruption," but believing also that he himself should share that blessedness and glory, for he sang also, "As for me, I shall behold Thy presence in righteousness: and when I awake up after Thy likeness I shall be satisfied with it."

But now, my brethren, it is certain that men think not so much of the operation of the Holy Ghost as they do of other spiritual matters. As the doctrine of the Trinity is the most difficult matter in our religion to conceive, so in the doctrine of the Trinity is the person and the office of the Holy Ghost. We can conceive of a Father, and a Son, when we cannot conceive of One who proceedeth from Them, and is equal to Them. Our ordinary notion of the relations of a family is no help to us here. We can conceive Him who, forasmuch as we are partakers of flesh and blood, Himself also took part of the same. We can conceive the Father, the brightness of whose glory the Son was, and the express image of His Person, when we fail to conceive concerning the Holy Spirit, whence it cometh and whither it goeth. Our reason and intelligence help us less concerning the Spirit as a Person than concerning the other Persons in the blessed Trinity. And yet it is more for want of meditation than for want of light in Holy Scripture to guide us; more for want of searching the Word than (reverently be it spoken) for any defect therein. And it may be one great and blessed use of this course of sermons —which have for their object the encouragement of deeper and fuller meditation on this part of the

Revelation of God—to turn men's thoughts more this way, and to teach them that indeed the higher contentments of our nature, which some men are pleased to imply cannot be found in theology as at present taught, need not be sought in deviations therefrom, or in refinement of speculation upon its simple verities, as though the spirit of enquiry could not rest satisfied in those verities as ordinarily received, (which is the whole temper of the present day); but that in strictest accordance with all that has been held in the Church for so many ages, (and which must either continue to be held, or an apostacy so terrible ensue as these men themselves would shrink from contemplating,) the investigation of the work of the Holy Ghost in the world and in ourselves, contains abundant matter for the greatest intellects that ever yet handled high and mysterious truths to exercise themselves on—abundant space wherein the grace of God, which we have in Christ Jesus our Lord, blending with our faculties, and tempers, and the dispositions and affections of our hearts, may grow and increase and fructify amazingly, to the establishment of the Church in such sort as by reason of her many defects the world hath not yet seen. Yea, it is by some growth and increase, tending probably in this direction, that the fulness of the Gentiles is to come in, and through that the blindness of Israel to be removed, and the veil that is still upon their hearts in the reading of the Old Testament to be taken away, and they to be received back again into the Church, and thereupon the great gathering in of the Gentiles to ensue, of which the Apostle saith, it shall be as "life from the dead." It is in speaking of this marvellous consummation that St. Paul uses the expression, "Now the Lord is that Spirit;" i.e. 'to whom are we to look for bringing about such unlooked for and glorious events? To the Lord! But Christ here is the Spirit of Christ. The Lord is that Spirit by whom this wondrous change shall be wrought; and in that universal freedom which shall then ensue, we all — we Gentiles — beholding as in a glass the glory of the Lord, shall be changed into the same image, from glory to glory, from one degree of glory to another, even as by the Lord the Spirit, i.e. the Holy Ghost; whose office it is, as the Author of all life and being, to regenerate, to renew, to sanctify and transform us into the image of God in Christ.'

In all these diversities of operation, therefore, we are bound, as intelligent readers of Holy Scripture, to recognise the Holy Ghost as the Giver of Life. From the day when He first moved upon the waters unto this day, He hath given to all this visible creation "life and breath and all things." Of quickening power we know by Revelation no other source than Him: no, nor have all the researches of reverent men—nor even of those who, vainly puffed up with the fleshly mind, have somewhat rashly intruded into things they have not seen—discovered any other. Men of science, worshipping the things they are conversant with, or something in them which they deem divine, by their own confession "worship they know not what." We know what we worship; for this is the very privilege of our salvation. We worship the Holy Ghost, the Giver of Life, believing with all our hearts that which is written; confessing that we cannot stir one step beyond that which is written, in so high and mysterious a matter, without peril of being ourselves bewildered and deceiving others. In this and all other things pertaining unto life, God has been pleased to reveal to us whatever is good and profitable for us to know. For the rest, we know to Whom to pray, and through Whom to pray, and from Whom to expect the things we pray for; meanwhile, with the help of the Holy Spirit, we search all things,—yea, so far as this light guideth us, even the deep things of God. In all the operations of nature, in all this visible world, in the starry heavens, in the moonlit sea, in the blaze of noon, in wind and storm, in snow and vapour, in herbs, and flowers, and trees, and in the tribes of living creatures that dwell in them, we see Him whom we worship. The Holy Ghost is all. All in the glorious universe we see, all in the things we cannot see; all in the world of sense, all in the world of spirits; all in the past and present, all in the future; all within us and without us,—is HE.

The Song of the Three Children, as it is called, expresses our imperfect adoration of the Creator

Spirit. But these are the least parts of His works. Our chiefest joy is to recognise His presence in the regeneration, whereby that which robbed the creation of its glory, the sin of man, is to be remedied, redressed, repaired, and the fallen creature to be renewed after the image of his Creator; in a word, as the Regenerator of the soul, as ever engaged in carrying on this work, from the day of Baptism until the day of death, fulfilling in each of God's elect that righteousness unto which he is called according to the foreknowledge of God the Father, through sanctification of the Spirit, unto obedience and sprinkling of the Blood of Jesus Christ. And when we think that not this only, but all things in order to this, are His work; that by Him every stone of the living temple is prepared, adjusted, and firmly laid; that every word spoken in truth is inspired by Him; that every wise counsel, every pure and worthy deed is from Him; that it is He who hath guided His people into all truth, and guarded them from all fatal and deadly error,—we have then, brethren, seen the whole work of the lifegiving Spirit in the world that now is, and we may understand in some measure why sin and blasphemy against the Holy Ghost is more unpardonable, seeing that all such have not only rejected the truth presented to them upon evidence which in earthly matters would be reckoned incontrovertible, but have also resisted, it can scarce be without consciousness of what they were doing, the power and influence of the Spirit of Life. Brethren, it is impossible, humanly speaking, but that some of you in the present unsettled state of opinion should have to pass through this form of temptation. May the Spirit of Life in Christ Jesus inform, enlighten, guide you; make you free, as in respect of other snares of the adversary, so in this also, from the law of sin and death; keep you firm and stedfast in the ancient faith and confession of the Church—"I believe in the Holy Ghost, the Lord and Giver of Life."

SERMON V.

The Grieving of the Spirit.

BY

A. P. STANLEY, D.D.,

REGIUS PROFESSOR OF ECCLESIASTICAL HISTORY, AND CANON OF
CHRIST CHURCH.

The Grieving of the Spirit.

EPHESIANS iv. 30.

"Grieve not the Holy Spirit of God."

WE all know the general terms in which the Bible sets forth the conflict going on between good and evil, between the Tempter and the tempted. But what is meant by this special warning of the Apostle, planted as it is in the midst of a series of the most homely and practical exhortations?

Two things are said in this short sentence. One is that we do wrong to "the Spirit," "the Holy Spirit," "the Spirit of God," (τὸ Πνεῦμα, τὸ Ἅγιον, τοῦ Θεοῦ); the other is that we do wrong to the Spirit of God by "grieving" Him, by causing Him sorrow.

To each of these points I desire to call your attention.

I. First, what is meant by the appeal of the Apostle, in this conflict of the soul, to *the Holy Spirit of God?* It is always instructive and edifying to ask why, in the Bible, one turn of expression is used rather than another, what is the reason of the preference of one phrase to another, seemingly of the same general intention. Most evidently is this the case in the sacred words which express the doctrine of the Holy Trinity.

From certain points of view, we see, we are told of nothing except the Love, the Power, the Providence, of our heavenly Father. From another point of view, we see, we are told of nothing except the Life, the Death, the Resurrection, the Character of our blessed Lord. From a third point of view, we see, we are told of nothing except the work and influence of the blessed Spirit. Each of the Three has indeed, so to speak, the same background:—"The Godhead of the Father, of the Son, and of the Holy Ghost is all one: the glory equal, the majesty co-eternal. Such as the Father is, such is the Son, and such is the Holy Ghost." But each Divine Object, as viewed by itself, seems for the moment to shut out from our view everything else. The description of each, whether we use the Latin name *Persona*, or the Greek name *Hypostasis*, is of sufficient substance and force to occupy the whole horizon of our vision. We have but to stand in one of three positions, and each of the Three for the moment represents to us the whole Godhead. It is in the third of these positions that we stand to-night, and during the whole course of these sermons. It is the third of these Divine Names on which I have to dwell; and I cannot sufficiently impress on theological students the importance of studying the exact force and meaning of the word, *the Spirit*, the *Holy Spirit*, as it is used throughout the Scriptures; significant always, but, in our own times, of absolutely peculiar significance. He who has thoroughly grasped what he means, or what he ought to mean, when he says, "I believe in the Holy Ghost," has obtained the master-key to the special difficulties, the true solution of the special questions of modern times and of the coming age.

The speculative applications of this great doctrine I reserve for other occasions. I confine myself now to the practical application made of it by the Apostle. What is meant when he refers us for our safeguard against evil, not to the love of the Father or to the grace of Christ, but to our communion with the Holy Spirit? He means this—That there is a power not out of ourselves, but within ourselves, resting on no external proof, but on its own internal evidence, deep-seated in our own innermost conscience and consciousness, which is no less than the power and presence of God Himself. Those good thoughts which dart across our souls we know not whence or how, those flashes of a better light than that which we meet in common every-day life, those tender emotions and noble instincts which shrink from the presence of everything base, or treacherous, or impure; that stern voice of conscience which rules, and condemns, and approves, what we do, and think, and say;—these are not the mere passing, fleeting results of this earthly human frame; they are the breathings, the messages, the expressions, the intimations of the near Presence of Almighty God, the Lord of heaven and earth. If we listen to them, we are on His side; if we refuse to listen to them, we place ourselves on the side, it may be, of success now, but of total, hopeless failure at the end. In that wonderful account of the first battle of the Crimean war[*], which many of us, I doubt not, have lately read, it is maintained that "the turning moment of a fight is a moment of trial for the soul, and not for the body; and it is therefore that such courage as men are able to gather from being gross in numbers can be easily outweighed by the warlike virtues of the few..... According to the grand thought which floated in the mind of the churchman who taught to the Russians" (so the historian of the battle draws out this remarkable thought) "their form of prayer for victory, there are Angels of Light and Angels of Darkness and Horror, who soar above the heads of the soldiery destined to be engaged in close fight, and attend them into battle. When the fight grows hot, the angels hover down near to earth, with their bright limbs twined deep in the wreaths of smoke which divides the combatants. But it is no coarse bodily help that these Angels bring. More spiritual than the old Immortals, they strike no blow, they snatch no man's weapon, they lift away no warrior in a cloud. What the Angel of Light can bestow is valour, priceless valour; a light to lighten the path to victory, giving men grace to see the bare truth, and, seeing it, to have the mastery. To troops who are to be blessed with victory, the Angel of Light

[*] Kinglake's History of the Invasion of the Crimea, i. 458.

seems to beckon and gently draw them forward to their destined triumph."

Such is the account given of an actual battle by an eyewitness, who had the genius to see into the inner causes of success and failure. But, if it be true of the conflict of physical forces in war, how much more is it true of the conflict of the moral forces in the soul. There, indeed, it is no external agency which will help us; it is the Holy Spirit of God working with and through our spirits. It is not on physical force, or worldly station, or applauding multitudes, no, nor even the oracles of human authority, however venerable, nor the advice and support of friends, however dear, that we must lean in the last resort. We must lean on God and on our own souls; on God in our own selves; that is, on all that is best and purest in ourselves; that is, on the strength and the light which can be given only by the indwelling of the Divine Spirit itself, not in the mere outer chambers of our opinions, or our manners, or our language, but in the very innermost sanctuary of all, our hearts, our consciences. Give us this, O God, and Thou givest us everything. Give us Thyself to enlighten, elevate, strengthen. Give us Thyself not in nature only, not in history only, not in Thy fatherly love only, not in Thy redeeming grace only, but in Thy close communion and fellowship with our own souls, and minds, and judgments. Make our wills strong with the strength of Thy will; make our hearts holy with the freshness of

Thy holiness; make our judgments independent with the independence of Thine own eternity; make our souls in their search for truth to be " safe under Thy feathers, for Thy faithfulness and Thy truth shall be our shield and buckler." This, and nothing less than this, we ask of Thee in all time of our tribulation, in all time of our wealth, in all our thirst for knowledge, in all our sense of ignorance, in the war which we have to fight, in the decision which we have to decide, in the solution which we hope to find for our thousand difficulties. This is what we have to seek. Within ourselves, not without ourselves, in the court of our own consciences, which is the throne of the Holy Spirit of God, must each decision be made for good or for evil in that struggle, which gives its true value to life and to death, across the dark river, and through the tangled thicket, and amidst the flying shots, and up to the distant height, where we shall stand at last victorious through the might of that blessed Spirit, which is indeed " our Refuge and Strength, our very present Help in trouble."

This, then, is the scene of our main conflict,—our own hearts and souls. This is the main support to which we must look,—God's Spirit working with, and through, and in, our spirits, by those gifts, and impulses, and breathings of moral strength and spiritual purity which are parts of His own essential nature.

II. And now comes the other word in the Apostle's warning. He describes, in a figure no doubt, but still in a figure full of life and force, how it is that this sacred Guest and Friend is, if I may so say, affected by the movements, the unconscious, unintentional movements, of our own hearts and spirits. "*Grieve* not the Holy Spirit of God." He does not say "Resist not the Spirit," or "Quench not the Spirit," or "Anger not the Spirit," though he might say all of these. He says, and this is the point to which I have to invite your thoughts, "*Grieve not* the Spirit."

Forgive me if I venture to explain this figure of the Apostle by an illustration which draws out in a living image the thought which lies hid in his emphatic phrase.

There is a well-known German picture, representing a young man playing at chess with the Tempter of his soul. He is intent on his game; his head is leaning on his hand; he sees only the moves of the pieces immediately before him; he thinks that he still has the play in his own grasp. Opposite to him sits the exulting Fiend: there is a look of triumph over the easy prey; already piece after piece has been taken: here a good deed is gone; there a prayer has been removed; there an act of faith; there an act of love; there an act of hope. A few more successful moves on the Tempter's side, and the game is won,—and the soul is lost.

But there is yet another Figure, which gives to the scene at once a deeper pathos and also a ray of hope. Behind the young man, unseen by him, unnoticed by the Tempter, stands the Guardian

Angel. The wings are spread for flight; the face is already turning away. It is a face not of anger, not of disappointment, not of despair, not of resistance, but of profound compassion and grief.

That picture represents to us well the state of many amongst ourselves; it represents also the meaning of the mournful, strange, almost singular expression of the Apostle, "Grieve not the Holy Spirit of God."

I have said that our condition is, or may be, like that of the young man in this familiar picture. We may see him in many forms, in many stages of life: not perhaps here in this church, or now at this moment; but often elsewhere, often before or hereafter. He is in the midst of his companions. He is the life and soul of the party. The guests are full of fun and play. The evening wears on, and the conversation and the mirth grows faster and louder: and then comes the very temptation of which the Apostle is speaking in the chapter which contains this warning,—"Corrupt communications." "Corrupt," ($\sigma\alpha\pi\rho\grave{o}\varsigma$): it may be only that worthless, rotten, foolish talk, which has no direct mischief, but which weakens, unnerves, dissolves the strength of our souls. "Corrupt:" it may be that darker, defiling current of ambiguous stories, and filthy jests, and loose songs, which gladly lend themselves to the ready lips of him who speaks, and are caught up gladly by the ready ears of those who hear. He plunges into this downward stream; he sees nothing but the excited faces of his hearers; he hears nothing but the peals of laughter which he calls forth. But behind that roar of merriment there is a sadness which is not of this earth. There is a sadness of the departing Angel of Light, to whom every word so uttered is a pang of misery. There is a sadness such as would cloud the brow of father, and mother, and sisters, were they there to hear; not anger, not even disgust, but deep, unutterable grief. There is a sadness which even in the intervals of this loud and wild talk pierces his own soul, and which breaks in upon him with a deadly faintness when the tables are cleared and the guests are gone, and he is left alone to think of the nonsense and filth with which he has polluted and degraded his own lips, or the friends whom those foolish, wicked words have misled, and wronged, and defiled, and corrupted.

Or shall we follow him a step further than words? Has that game still gone on? Has the Tempter carried off not words only but acts? Has the young man, still unconscious, still with his head as it were between his hands, still thinking no evil, still meaning no mischief,—has he been led across the fatal threshold? Has he been plunged not only into words, but deeds of darkness—dark, deep, entangling sins, which drag on a long train behind of concealment, and extravagance, and misery, and shame? There are many warnings that might be used. But I repeat this one of the Apostle. Think not of the disgrace, or the defilement, or the loss,— but think of the *grief*, of the *sorrow* that follows. Think of the sadness, deepening, and ever deepening still, on those beloved faces of which I spoke before,—of father, mother, brother, sister. Think of the pang which will shoot across your own soul, in the sudden shock that rouses you at night, or the first bitter waking thought of the morning. That sadness, those pangs, are but the shadows of the sadness which broods over the Holy Spirit and Mind of God, as He sees the work of His hands destroyed, as word after word and act after act disfigures, corrupts, and ruins the spirit which was His appointed dwelling-place.

Or look at another scene. Most perhaps of those who hear me would turn a deaf ear to those temptations of which the Apostle speaks. But there is another game which the Tempter can play. The young man is yet more unconscious than before,—of easy good-nature, of high generous spirit, perhaps of great capacities, of grand hopes, and great opportunities. He is there,—he sits in his room,—surrounded with comforts and luxuries. Hour after hour comes and goes, and he cares not to use them. All these golden Oxford years, which contain the promise of his future usefulness, are stolen away from him by the Enemy, not through vice, not through mischief, but through sheer indolence, and reckless idleness. He lounges from room to room; he leans out of his window; he hangs by his door; he loiters by the street, or the gate, or the quadrangle; and piece by piece, year by year, term by term, and week by week, those precious hours are snatched away, and he leaves this place worse educated, worse instructed than he came; he enters on life worse prepared for its trials than had he never set foot within these walls. He looks back on nothing mournful, or disgraceful, or painful; all seems to have been easy, and sunny, and joyous. So it seems. But is there not here also a sadness, a grief in the background? not, as in the former case, sharp, acute, and piercing, but yet a sadness which creeps even over our earthly friends and our own memories, when we think what labour, what care, what money has been spent on our education, and spent, alas! almost wholly in vain; a sadness which in its fulness can only belong to that Divine Mind, which sees the future as well as the present, which sees with the vividness of omniscience what we might have been and what we are not. Ἐχθιστὴ ὀδύνη,—the bitter grief which sees the evil which it cannot repair, and which it cannot prevent. For we cannot repair the loss of the irrevocable past, and to restore that past to us is the one task which, as the ancients said, even God Himself cannot accomplish.

Or go a step higher yet. There are those who have yet greater destinies, and whose lives seem even now, in some measure, to correspond to those destinies. There is the youth blameless in act, zealous in study,—with a mind or with a character which, if all go well, must exercise an ennobling, elevating influence over the circle in which he will hereafter be placed; over the prospects, it may be, of the whole coming generation.

Rejoice in him; hope for him.

But here, also, the Tempter has his hand on the chessboard. That blameless, gentle youth gets entangled in the meshes of some absorbing enthusiasm, or one-sided system; or he shuts himself up within some narrow circle; or he unwinds for himself unconsciously, almost mechanically, those cords which bind him to God or to his brethren: he drops, if he be of a mere intellectual turn of mind, the blessed charities of home, or the blessed moments of morning and evening prayer, or those exalting, invigorating, soothing influences of the more sacred ordinances of Christendom, from which few, very few, can part without feeling a deep and serious loss; or he breaks away, if he be of another disposition, from the genial intercourse with his fellow men; he learns to despise his old friends; he looks with suspicion, jealousy, irritation, on all that is better, and freer, and grander than that which falls within his immediate vision.

And so the ardent student dwindles away into a captious, critical cynic; and so the kind, loving, gentle, humble companion of our youth grows up into a hard, narrow, supercilious dogmatist; and so the generous philanthropist stiffens into a worldly, eager, bitter partisan; and he whose mind was once open to all the approaches of truth,—to whom truth was once dearer than any worldly interests, or any selfish aims, or any cherished fancies,—loses his hold upon it; he becomes satisfied with any argument, however feeble, in behalf of what he wishes; he becomes indifferent to any consideration, however noble, which disturbs or contradicts his accustomed habits of thought or life.

And so God's work which should have been done by these, or the like of these, and which can be done by no one else, is left undone, and the world and the Church groan and pine for them, and groan and pine in vain. Surely "this too is vanity and vexation of spirit;"—vexation and grief to the spirit of man, but vexation and grief, multiplied a hundred-fold, to the Holy Spirit of God. A lost opportunity; a lost life; a loss which, in the sight of God, leaves a scar on the face of the whole generation,—this is indeed a blow to the Spirit of Truth, and the Spirit of Goodness. We do indeed, as we come across such cases as these, seem to hear not indeed the one piercing lament that mourns over one lost soul, but something which is more pathetic still,—" the long sorrowful wailing sound" which is described, after a hard-fought battle, " as though it had been wrung from the heart of brave men defeated [b];" the tokens observed with bitter grief by the historian of the last days of Jerusalem, the awful signs of departing Deity, when through the Temple courts was heard, or thought to be heard, the motion, the sad despairing cry, as of a great multitude, saying "Let us go hence."

I have dwelt on this side of the conflict between good and evil, because the text invites it, and because it is well for a moment to be recalled not

[b] Kinglake's History of the Invasion of the Crimea, ii. 332.

merely to the serious, but to the tragical side of human sin; to be reminded not only of the anger and the love, but the grief of Him whose Spirit is not merely despised and outraged, but vexed and grieved, as with a father's or a mother's grief, as, one by one, His armies of good thoughts, and noble words, and just intentions, seem to be withdrawn or driven off either from the individual soul or from the collective spirit of man. "The Lord *repented* that He had made man, and it *grieved* Him at His heart." Deduct from this expression all that you will of figure, metaphor, and analogy, yet still it remains a sublime and pathetic expression of one side of the Divine Nature and of the Divine Providence. Not once only, but often in the course of history, must this Divine repentance have brooded over the world, and the Heart of God been grieved at the failure of the noblest characters, at the waste of the fairest opportunities, at the relapse and retrogression of a whole nation, a whole generation, a whole race of mankind from the mission which lay before them.

"My Spirit shall not always strive[c] with man." Such is the result which the sacred writer ascribes to this awful Penitence of God. These great opportunities for good come once in a man's life, and do not return. They come once in a century, nay, we may almost say, they come once only in an age. The generation, the century, the age itself, may be

[c] Gen. vi. 3, 6. The substance of this will be true in whatever way we interpret the Hebrew word translated "strive."

like that unconscious victim of the Tempter's arts. It may oppose to the Spirit of God no violent resistance, nothing but the force of inertness, of inactivity, of incapacity, the *vis inertiæ* of human nature. But the effect is the same. "The Spirit is grieved," "vexed [d]," thwarted, driven away by the unsympathetic, unrecognising, unconscious opposition, and the opportunity comes no more. These, and such as these, are the sad freaks of human nature that make angels weep. This, and such as this, was the prospect which drew tears from the eyes of Him whose Spirit we seek to win. "He, when He beheld the city, wept over it, and said, If thou hadst known, even thou, at least in this thy day, the things which belong to thy peace! but now they are hid from thine eyes [e]."

This, then, is the lesson which I wish to leave upon your minds,—the sorrow, the profound grief, which strikes here and there, even in places where you least expect it, even into the very Heart of God, even into the very counsels of His Providence, even into the very movements and yearnings of His Spirit, by your undesigned, unconscious, unintentional omission, ignorance, forgetfulness, apathy, pre-occupation, prejudice, want of presence of mind, want of forethought, want of care for yourselves or for others.

The time is coming when you will be sorry for it. You have spread sorrow far and wide already; at last it will reach yourself.

[d] Isa. lxiii. 10.   [e] Luke xix. 42.

Yet I would not so leave the subject altogether. For, if you can grieve the Spirit of God, you can also rejoice the Spirit of God.

Even that long, sorrowful wail, of which I spoke before in the battles of earthly warfare, is not without hope,—"it is the cry of those who are not content to yield." And so much more in spiritual warfare. There is the rush of joy in your own hearts and in the courts of Heaven, when you have recovered your lost game: there is the joy which irradiates the faces of all whom you know and love when the prodigal returns, when the angels welcome back the penitent sinner[f]: there is a deep joy which reaches up from man to God, and down from God to man, when the courageous rebuke or the silent look has put to shame the filthy jest or the ill-natured sarcasm; or when the idle, careless, spendthrift youth shuts his door against intruders, and turns over a new leaf, and makes good use of the time that still remains to him; or when the blamelessness and guilelessness of youth grows up stedfastly along with the honest, mature, sincere mind of the full-grown man; or when an unexpected sorrow, or trial, or vicissitude of life once more opens the soul to the returning Spirit of Holiness; or when the reading of a new book, or the question of an innocent child, or the inquiry of a simple peasant, tears asunder the veil which kept out the Spirit of Truth.

Then we see the true happiness of man, then we

[f] Luke xv. 10, 24.

perceive the joy of angels; then we recognise (if we may so say) the happiness and the joy of God. Look at such an one—look at that constant, serene, cheerful, open countenance. Listen to his free, hearty, genial laugh. See how the cares, and perplexities, and doubts of this world pass by him as though they concerned him not. See how from the real griefs and sorrows of earth he draws new strength, new comfort, new life. This is indeed "joy in the Holy Ghost:" this is the joy that transfigures the outward man, because it comes from the joy of the Eternal Spirit within: this is the exuberant, overflowing joy of the Psalmist, when he emerges even out of the depths of crime and sin,—"Be glad in the Lord, and rejoice, ye righteous: and shout for joy, all ye that are upright in heart[g]." "Cast me not away from Thy Presence: and take not Thy Holy Spirit from me. O give me the comfort of Thy help again: and stablish me with Thy Free Spirit[h]."

[g] Ps. xxxii. 11. [h] Ps. li. 11, 12.

SERMON VI.

The Sin against the Holy Ghost.

BY

T. T. CARTER, M.A.,
RECTOR OF CLEWER.

The Sin against the Holy Ghost.

ST. MATTHEW xii. 31, 32.

"Wherefore I say unto you, All manner of sin and blasphemy shall be forgiven unto men: but the blasphemy against the Holy Ghost shall not be forgiven unto men. And whosoever speaketh a word against the Son of Man, it shall be forgiven him: but whosoever speaketh against the Holy Ghost, it shall not be forgiven him, neither in this world, neither in the world to come."

ONE of Satan's chiefest snares is to make the soul distrust the mercies of God. Where he fails to produce disobedience, he may cause distrust, or doubt, or despondency. He may make the soul of the righteous sad, whom God has not made sad, and thus open the way to further temptations, to loss of energy, to distaste for prayer, to fears that dishonour God, to recklessness, or indifference, destroying effort and hindering the way of perfection, checking the soul's advance where he cannot destroy. Or if such temptations fail, he may work such overpowering sadness, such dark despair, as to make religion an intolerable burden, and scare away many who shun the melancholy sight, checking in others the desire of a religious life, though the saddened soul itself may still faithfully cling to its once bright hope more precious even in its present gloom than all that the world can offer.

There is no text which has been more commonly employed,—for the prince of infidelity and wickedness will clothe himself in armour of light,—no text has been more commonly employed as a weapon thus to slay or wound the fearful soul, than this. Few there are who have not at times trembled at it, who have not asked, Is it I? Some have gone on their way, unable to solve the awful doubt. Some have even died with its terror harrowing their conscience to the very last. How constantly has the guide of souls to seek to give assurance that the text is misapplied, and the fear utterly vain!

And yet there must be cases where this text does apply, or it would not be written in the Word of Truth; it would not have issued out of the lips of Christ. Nor could it be meant to be limited to the Jews, or to that one generation. There is no restriction to any special people in the "*whosoever* blasphemeth;" it is a world-wide term that is used to denote the possibly guilty one. And indeed the words imply that this fearful doom could not be fulfilled in its extreme sense at the time it was spoken; for the Holy Ghost was not yet given, and the full blasphemy against the Holy Ghost could not precede His full manifestation. The words, when spoken, were a warning before the time of its possible fulfilment, not a threat of its immediate judgment. Nor, again, can it be limited to the times immediately succeeding the coming of the Holy Ghost; for as the dispensation of the Spirit extends to all time, so must the possible sin against Him extend also to all time. It is left on the page of Holy Scripture, as a declaration of terror which cannot pass away, and must be intended to work in the soul a healthful spirit of holy fear, like the bounds about the Mount, set there lest the fire should break through and consume; but to be cleared of all doubt, lest it should hinder perfect peace where God has willed peace. And indeed this very text ought to ensure peace. There is no text in the Scriptures so full of love and hope, notwithstanding all its cause of terror; for while it speaks of the blasphemy which shall not be forgiven, "neither in this world, nor in the world to come," it at the same time says; "All manner of sin and blasphemy," "All blasphemies wherewith soever men shall blaspheme*," however long continued, however profane, saving only this one, "shall be forgiven unto men."

St. Augustine has said of this text, that "there is not in all the Holy Scriptures found a more important or more difficult question;" and he confesses that he had "always in his discourses to the people avoided the difficulty and embarrassment of it, though he had not been negligent in asking and seeking and knocking; and only at last, one day, as he listened to this lesson, and heard this gospel read, there was such a beating at his heart that he believed it was God's will, that the people should

* St. Mark iii. 28.

hear something on this subject by his ministry;" and then he expounded it [b]. So great is the need then which we have, brethren, of the special aid of God in venturing now on such a subject, which according to the order of this series, not of our own seeking, but of the mind of one set over us, has been appointed for this evening.

The true interpretation of this momentous text is to be found, not in viewing it by itself alone, but in viewing it in connexion with its context, nay more, in connexion with the entire revelation of God. For this, the one only utterly hopeless state of man, cannot be viewed as a single sin, and so taken separately, but as a whole and complex state; not a single offence, but the entire antagonism to the entire revelation of mercy; and therefore as extensive in its bearings as the revelation itself, as the undoing of the whole work of Christ, as the counteraction of the full predestination of God's love for man. Like some dark orb in space, wholly eclipsing the sun, so this fearful doom traverses the face of Holy Scripture, and as it passes across our vision, shuts out all light and hope and love. It is the state described by St. Paul, which it was "impossible to renew unto repentance [c];" it is "the sin unto death [d]" of St. John; the state "devilish, having not the Spirit [e]" of St. Jude.

Let us therefore view this text in this its wide

---

[b] St. Aug., Homilies on the New Testament, Serm. xxxi.; Library of the Fathers, vol. xvi. p. 172.
[c] Heb. vi. 4—6.   [d] St. John v. 16.   [e] St. Jude 19.

bearing. The Holy Scriptures reveal to us the existence of a state of creatures who have finally rejected God, rejected Him deliberately, with a full knowledge of Him whom they have rejected, with a desperate perversion of their being, alienated from God and from a desire after God, hopelessly for ever. Such is the state of devils, to whom is "reserved the blackness of darkness for ever[f]." They have rejected and blasphemed God in the full light and consciousness of God, with a hopeless obduracy. Such a state may be reproduced in man; it is the Satanic life; not like the first fall of man, the yielding to temptation through weakness, but the deliberate choice of evil and hardened hatred of all that is of God.

The possibility of such a state in man appears throughout the Holy Scriptures. There have been three dispensations since the early patriarchal period, and under each dispensation the warning of such a state is given. In the first covenant, the Law, there was no forgiveness for blaspheming the Name of Jehovah. That covenant revealed the unity, the essential essence of Godhead, and therefore to reject this truth was to reject all the light which that covenant gave. There was forgiveness for sin under the first covenant, through the anticipated virtue of the promised atonement; but there was no such forgiveness for this blasphemy. It was the absolute final rejection of all that the covenant contained, and of Him Who gave it. "Thou shalt

[f] St. Jude 13.

speak unto the children of Israel, saying, Whosoever curseth his God shall bear his sin. And he that blasphemeth the name of the Lord, he shall surely be put to death, and all the congregation shall certainly stone him: as well the stranger, as he that is born in the land, whosoever blasphemeth the name of the Lord, shall be put to death [g]."

This sentence was but the prophetic type of a yet greater guilt, as the Mosaic covenant was but a type of a better revelation. As the better revelation was given, so a yet more awful blasphemy appears. When the revelation of the Son of Man was given, then appeared the possibility of man blaspheming God even when manifested before his eyes in the flesh. Such blasphemy was the special sin of the dispensation of the Son of Man. This sin was indicated by our Lord when He said of the Jewish leaders; "If I had not come and spoken unto them, they had not had sin: but now they have no excuse for their sin [h]." It was not meant that they had no sin, in any sense of the term, but that they had not *the* sin, the sin of rejecting Him, rejecting the Godhead manifest in the flesh, the sin of obduracy in finally rejecting this fuller revelation of Divine love.

But yet even this rejection of the Son of Man was but a type, a forerunner of the completed and hopelessly final condemnation of man; for the rejection of our Lord was pardonable. The dispensation of the Son of Man was not the final dispensation of

[g] Levit. xxiv. 15, 16.   [h] St. John xv. 22.

mercy, and therefore the doom of its rejection was not final. There was a revelation of God yet to come, a revelation more fully manifesting the Divine Nature; and therefore there was yet to come the complete condemnation which admitted no more hope, no more pleading for sins. The dispensation of the Spirit was to succeed the dispensation of the Son of Man; and then, and only then, fell the full doom of a judgment, which was to close the door for ever against the possibility of forgiveness, whether "in this world, or in the world to come." This final dispensation was yet to come, when our Lord uttered the words of the text, and therefore the final doom He pronounced, was yet to come[1].

The Jews of old bordered upon this unpardonable

---

[1] Some of the Fathers thought that our Lord was here speaking of a sin at the time committed, and expressed in its fulness in the saying of the Pharisees. Thus St. Athanasius:— "The Saviour when before He rebuked them for many sins, yet exhorted them to repent; but when they said, 'He casteth out devils by Beelzebub,' He speaketh of this no longer as a sin, but as blasphemy so great, that on those who dared this, punishment must come, without escape and pardon." Thus, too, St. Jerome:—"He who sees My mighty works, and reviles Me who am the Word of God, and says that the works of the Holy Spirit, working by Me, are the works of Beelzebub, hath no forgiveness;"—quoted by Wordsworth *in loc.*

The analogy, however, of the successive dispensations, as well as the contrast involved in the passage of the text between the Son of Man and the Holy Ghost, seem to coincide with the view supported by the authority of St. Augustine, and adopted in this sermon, though the completed sin may by implication have been then committed. Perhaps the two apparently different views are thus to be reconciled.

sin, when they blasphemed the Name of Jehovah. The Jews in our Lord's day bordered upon it, when they blasphemed the Son of Man. We know not how far either of these two blasphemies involved the individual soul guilty of them in the further guilt which was foretold. Their sin in either case may by implication have reached the full, the complete malignity of the extreme and final guilt; but this final guilt was not as yet the revealed doom, not as yet the penalty of the dispensation then vouchsafed, because as yet the dispensation of the Spirit was not come. The final doom was the rejection of the final dispensation.

It is to be carefully noted, that not every blasphemy against the Holy Ghost is in the text spoken of, but "*the* blasphemy," thus marking a special and distinctive sin. When the atonement was accomplished, and the Spirit speaking in St. Peter called the Jews to repentance, there was no limit assigned to the possibility of forgiveness open to them for their sins past. Even those who ascribed our Lord's miracles of healing to an evil spirit, thus blaspheming the Spirit in Him, could be forgiven. Even the crucifixion of the Lord of Glory, the seeking to destroy and cast out, as far as this act of extremest guilt availed, the very Spirit Who abode in Him,—even this could be forgiven. Only afterwards was to come the completed blasphemy against the Holy Ghost, which could not be, till the Holy Ghost was revealed; and, therefore, " he that speaketh a word against the Son of Man, it shall be forgiven him: but whosoever speaketh against the Holy Ghost,"—the full revelation of the Holy Ghost,—" it shall not be forgiven him, neither in this world, neither in the world to come [k]." The dispensation of the Holy Ghost was the last dispensation of God, and therefore it, and it alone, had the doom of final and hopeless condemnation.

Nor is it merely because the dispensation of the Spirit is the last, that therefore, to use the language of St. Augustine [l], "the persevering hardness of the impenitent heart" against it is hopelessly unpardonable, but also because of the character of this dispensation. More close to the soul, more intimate, more full, more inwardly working in and upon our nature, is the Presence of the Spirit. He is equally the Spirit of the Father and of the Son, and where He is, They Both are. Therefore His Presence is the completion of the Presence combined of the ever-blessed Trinity. It is through the Spirit that Christ enters into us. It is the Spirit Who specially is the Indweller in human hearts. He is the convincer of sin. He is the illuminator of the mind. He is within us "the well of water springing up unto everlasting life." He is the consecrator of the Body of Christ, whether in the collective communion of the saints, or in the individual member. His is "the unction" of the Holy One, by which we "know all things." His is the active energy, and

[k] St. Matt. xii. 32.
[l] St. Aug., Serm. xxi.; Library of Fathers, vol. xvi. p. 182, ad fin.

the inward light, and the Divine consolation. He is the revealer of the hidden things of God to the soul. He is the witness that "witnesseth with our spirit." He re-creates, He renews, He is the seal impressing the mind, the being of God. He intercedes within us with the voice that cannot be uttered. He is the bond of the living bridal union between the soul and her Lord.

Therefore to reject the work of the Spirit, "the persevering hardness of an impenitent heart" fully set against Him when fully revealed in the final dispensation, is to reject not only the last revelation of Divine love, but also the more inner Presence with a closer working of a clearer light, a more complete Manifestation. It argues a stronger will for evil, a greater obduracy, a more impenetrable hardness of conscience, a colder heart, a more settled determination of a more fixed enmity against God, as well as a wilful closing up of the last door of hope. If all the gracious movements, and influences, and strivings, and convictions, and allurements, and terrors, and misgivings, and holy aspirations, and tender wooings, and illuminations and suggestions, which with unceasing flow, as "the wind blowing where it listeth," breathe over and within the soul, as an abiding Presence making Itself heard and felt in recesses of being where no human voice can reach, no human contact can approach,—if all this avail not, if the regenerate soul is proof throughout the whole period of its probation, and to the very close of its season of trial, against all such impressions ever renewed with unwearied long-suffering; or if ever acted on by them has again hardened itself with renewed energy of evil against them; and this continues to the very moment at which the soul passes within the veil, yea and beyond the veil, within the mysteries of other worlds, abiding still in the same obdurate antagonism to the whole manifestation of God,—then hath come "the blasphemy" which knows not, and never can know, the sweetness of the forgiveness of God; it is sealed with an eternal malignity against all the appealing tenderness of Divine compassion, or rather is only the more obdurately hardened by the infinite manifestations everywhere abounding of the truth and justice of God, of His mercy and His love.

In some pictures which represent the Last Supper the painter has not ventured to depict the form of Judas. He has left an empty seat, on which a garment is flung, and immediately beneath opens a dark chasm, where no form is seen. But the imagination fills up the picture, and follows the departed traitor, as he went forth in haste, when "it was night." Even so along the track of the history of the Church there are some on whom their own generation looked, as men thus hopelessly given over, sealed unto death in an amazing hardihood of hatred against the truth, of personal resistance to God; monuments, as far as human eye could discern, of the unpardonable sin. To speak with certainty in such cases who can dare? How or when God may vouchsafe repentance; what measure of repentance may grow out of secret germs here undiscovered, and be developed in the countless ages of other worlds into a complete reconciliation with God; what possibility of such an after term of advancement there may be arising out of the least faintest desires of the first workings of good in this world, who can venture to judge? But we can tell, and this with certainty, who have *not* committed the unpardonable sin, and who in their present state exhibit no tendencies to such a state. They who grieve with the apprehension of being thus reprobate, cannot possibly have fallen into it, from the very fact of their grieving; for they manifestly have at heart at least the wish, the desire of penitence, and the unpardonable sin is irreconcilable with even the faintest movement of repentance. They, too, who fear lest they should some day fall into this sin, have the surest safeguard against it in this very fear. They too who though continually falling into sin yet continually mourn over it, from the very fact that they thus feel their falling, cannot have sinned with this sin of blasphemy; for they have the consciousness of sin, the absence of which is one of its essential features. Nor can we say even of any one most hardened in his opposition to God, and given over to wilful iniquity, that he has committed the unpardonable sin; for where there is time for repentance, there is hope of repentance; and who knoweth of any man whether he may not yet turn and repent? And yet assuredly this terrible doom is not to be dismissed from our minds as though none had cause to fear; or as though it were not needful to arm ourselves against the possibility of approaching so terrible an end; for though we may escape the entire guilt, yet we may contract some measure of its malignity—we may come within its shadow. There are manifold degrees in evil, and even the least degree of such a Satanic alienation from God, of such a tendency in the soul, is beyond measure terrible to conceive. Unspeakably dreadful is the faintest possibility of any seed of such ungodliness developing more fully in another world, where habits will become more intense, and tendencies will reach their final stage, and the distinctions between good and evil will be seen in their full consummation, either of blessed conformity with God, or of variance with Him.

There are grievings of the blessed Spirit, infinite, far short of the unpardonable sin, which may never arrive at such a development, but yet which may partake of its character, which may in the eyes of God be identified with it, as a fruit of the same evil root, as possible forerunners of it, as types on which the fearful image of blasphemy is stamped, forming a likeness with those, whosoever they may be, who lie under the uttermost curse. We cannot doubt that the terrible warning is given in mercy as well as in judgment, that the elect, the children of His love, may learn to keep far away from the fearful vision, fleeing from even the faintest shadow of such a blackness of darkness, avoiding the very least kindred fellowship with such a state of utter hatred and alienation from God, as one would hasten to extinguish the feeblest spark of fire, when explosive materials are close at hand, and one's home and all dear to oneself within reach of its possible ravages. One part of a living faith, one sure sign of a soul right with God, one necessary token of acceptance, is the fear of offence, the childlike shrinking from the very least approach to any utterly forbidden thing. One mark of a true love and of a growing tendency to union with our Lord, is to take earnest heed against every remotest thought or inclination of the soul, which in the sight of God might wear even the faintest resemblance to the hated object. Love would put away from itself in the sight of the loved one every imaginable memorial of a state, which to the Divine Heart must be the *one* brooding sorrow above all sorrow, as it is the *one* sin which is beyond the influences of the precious Blood, beyond the reach of all sacrifice to atone or reconcile.

No one, moreover, fell at once into extreme sin. Small as a man's hand, as a speck on the horizon, is the cloud in which a prophet's eye can read the sweeping hurricane, the "sound of the abundance of rain." Not by one heedless indulgence is a whole life of the regenerate extinguished. Not at the beginnings of alienation from God are all the workings of earlier purer faith and love finally stamped out of a soul. Mostly by insidious, indirect, unconsidered approaches steals on the darkening of the holy light. Very slight are the first gradual weakenings of the bonds of love, which nevertheless tend to final separation. To be keenly sensitive, therefore, to the least suspicion, or fear of the first admittance of aught that bears a trace of the one unpardonable sin, must be a sure mark of the faith of God's elect.

And there are lesser faults which have been ever regarded as indications of possible approach to this fatal doom of blasphemy. Such, e. g., is the impugning, or even making light of, known truth. Even the least truth is the presence of the Spirit in the soul, for God is Truth, and everything leading to the truth is of His precious love, and is a seed of His eternal life. Such too is an obstinate purpose to continue in any grievous sin, when known to be sin; and even a carelessness about such continuance partakes of the same character; for each conviction of sin is a work of the Holy Ghost, a direct revelation of His presence in one of His most vital workings in our restoration, as the Reprover of sin. Such too is the presuming on God's mercy, it may be the venturing on a course which He forbids, or the neglect of His warnings, or the wilfulness that would force Him to follow one's own devices rather than obey His, or the obstinacy that would tempt Him to leave one to oneself, disregarding His loving care. Such too. is the untruthful concealment of sin which He has stirred the soul to confess, keeping it back; or the loving to dwell on the remembrance of some sin, feeding on its images, thus letting it keep its deadly hold over the heart; sparing and indulging oneself in the allowed consciousness of what God hates, thus suffered to stand between God and oneself in one's own soul, as the "abomination of desolation" standing in the holy place; or even the trifling with it, as though its stain injured us not. Such too is the continued resistance to the pleadings of the Spirit to advance higher, the clinging to the death of one's old nature, the refusal to accept the gracious stirrings mercifully interposed between oneself and the evil one, the preference of one's own way to His way, the Barabbas choice rather than the choice of Jesus as one's life and aim and desire, the slothful unwillingness to correspond with His loving movements within us, to acknowledge His claims over every region of one's soul, the keeping back part of the price of our Saviour's purchase which the Holy Ghost manifests Himself on Christ's behalf to claim for Him as His own, thus counteracting the effects of the combined love of the ever-blessed Trinity in their common seeking to transform the lost one, and renew His faded image in His redeemed. Such, again, is the denial of the grace of the Spirit in others, the joining in evil suspicions, unjust judgments, reckless condemnations, hasty calumnies or reports, the imputing false motives, questioning the realities of grace, countenancing mere popular dislikes or disparagements or unreasonable outcries, with loss of reverence and breach of charity, without fear, without humility, perhaps to the dishonour of God, or even feeding self-exaltation at the cost of the honour of God, indulging envy at His gifts in others, grieving souls wherein He would shed peace, and hindering His work, which He would accomplish through His own chosen instruments. Such too is the indifference to lesser sins, as though they mattered not; the saying to oneself in the soul,— "It is a little matter after all; how can God heed such small things? Why so much said about such a trifle? Are there not thousands of greater sins freely indulged around me? Why molest me in such a slight indulgence?" And yet if God has in any way pointed out this one thing as evil in His sight; if God has counted this small thing enough to awaken His efforts to work conviction within thy soul; if a revelation has been vouchsafed to thee on this very point; if, too, there may be many other lesser faults as yet undiscerned, and the removal of this is the condition of further light; if, too, the indulgence of this small thing causes a relaxation in the whole soul, indisposes it to spiritual acts, enfeebles prayer, destroys energy, opens the way to further incursions of Satan, prevents progress, stays increasing illuminations, is gradually forming into a habit, and is all the while grieving the Holy Spirit, how different must be its estimate in the mind of God and thine own, and how much more fatal its consequences than the first heedless thought discerned them to be! Such too must be the delay of penitence; the putting off the necessary change, or act of restitution; the thinking to find for oneself the more convenient season, as though the spirit of contrition would wait one's own time, and come when oneself wills; the keeping up to the last time the sins ever growing of years as they pass, till impenitence become a habit, and procrastination is an allowed state, an established impulse, and the fear of sin is more and more lessened by its continuance. Such too must be a negligence as to the means which the Holy Ghost has ordained for His manifestations, and through which He would come and fulfil His work of love and restoration—lack of diligence in prayer; of the study of prayer as the science of communion with the Unseen; of careful preparation of heart for holy ordinances; of reverence in the churches; of care to understand what one says, and professes, and acts before God; of devoutness in act and tone; of longings for more as we become prepared for more of the Divine communications, of the sealing of the sacred gifts; the lack of earnest discipline to cleanse the soul through the divinely chosen means by which the Holy Ghost remits sin in His Church; the omitting the one thing which He suggests to the soul as the possible means of communicating His love; more especially the delay of seeking Him in the blessed Sacrament of the Body and Blood of our Lord; or neglect of careful and constant thanksgiving, as valuing His gifts, as desiring to return back to the

Giver the only offering we have to make, the praises of one who has been blessed, and would bless in return. If the ordained array of Sacramental forms be indeed of God, as the framework for the Invisible to clothe Himself withal, and to take shape, that He may reveal and impart Himself,—then indeed how must every neglect of these things be a very opposing of the Divine presence and purposes within the very centre of our being!

But rather instead of leaving it to be a question, whether or no we are denying, or opposing, or shrinking from the movements and revelations of the Spirit of the living God, ought we not, would it not be the true instinct, the only faithful longing of the child-heart of the elect, to seek the utmost development of His free Spirit, to be even forward to attain fresh graces, to make ever-increasing advances to cover the multitude of sins past with greater charity, to correspond more and more with the gracious onward movements of love, to watch more and more intently for the gentle accents of the still small voice, to be ever arising at the ever-renewed merciful calls, to long to know more and more, and to love more and more, and to do more and more, and, if it be so, to suffer more and more, to look on each grace already given as only the incitement to advance, the condition of increased faithfulness, to desire with longings more and more unquenchable for ever-growing union with God. If these, His first gifts be so fair, so sweet, so congenial to one's higher aspirations, what must be the yet higher manifestations, what must be the promised recompense of faithfulness in the fervour of the first love, what the inner heart of love, when its first wooings are so winning, so attractive!

Rather, then, let a largeness of desire, with this determination of onward progress, be the sure, the acceptable mode of shunning the unpardonable sin; rather let a loving, earnest stretching forward be the way of securing oneself from the terrible doom, and not the attempt to stay oneself up from backward fallings; rather the reaching out to things that are before, than the vain hope of security in lingering on the debatable borders of what is lawful. Rather labour and be diligent, that wherever the soul feels itself most weak, there to strengthen it; whatever graces are the most feeble and failing, those be most sure to increase; and pray that the love of sanctity may grow with the desires of a deepening contrition, and wherever in times past one has failed, there to seek the implanting of the needed graces, thus making one's very faults the occasions of giving greater glory to our God. Rather let the onward movement of the regenerate spirit be one of hopeful aspiration, than of fear and trembling, the waiting with the ever-ready response for the ever-ready manifestation of love passing all understanding, the wondrous meeting of the Spirit with our spirit in the mutual consciousness of a common life, and responsive longings after a perfected union. And this Eternal

Voice ceases not to speak in our hearts. "The Spirit and the Bride say, Come. And let him that heareth say, Come. And let him that is athirst come. And whosoever will, let him take the water of life freely [m]."

[m] Rev. xxii. 17.

SERMON VII.

The Spirit convincing of Sin.

BY

THE LORD BISHOP OF LONDON.

The Spirit convincing of Sin.

MARK vi. 16.

"But when Herod heard thereof, he said, It is John, whom I beheaded: he is risen from the dead."

CONSCIENCE has two offices—it tells us to do what is right, it reminds us that we have done what is wrong. In both the Holy Spirit of God also works. The natural conscience performs both offices in a degree, but very imperfectly; the enlightened Christian conscience performs both more perfectly. I am to speak now especially of the conviction of sin wrought not by the natural conscience, but by grace. The two are interwoven, yet have they great differences. What is the knowledge of our duty suggested by the natural conscience compared with that clear intimation of the right which is revealed to the enlightened Christian conscience? And so also, what are those uneasy feelings on account of mistakes, and faults, and even crimes, which the natural conscience suggests, compared with the deep contrition of the Christian heart? Now we have before us in the text a wicked worldly man, whose natural conscience was stirred and no wonder, for he had committed a murder—a foul deliberate murder; not the less detestable because it was perpetrated with a certain pretence of principle; at least such principle as wicked worldly men acknowledge, more respectful to the opinions of those about them than to any fixed rules of right. We read "for his oath's sake" partly, but more really "for their sakes which sat about him," Herod consented to the petition of Herodias' daughter, and ordered the executioner to do his work. Now this Herod Antipas, though, like most of the others who bore his name, he was, as we all know, a very bad man, and did many bad things, living in adultery or incest with his brother Philip's wife,—still, like other bad men, he was not altogether bad, he had natural good feelings; besides, he had received sound religious instruction as a Jew, so that he could not fail to know much as to what was right, neither could he fail to have some uneasy feelings if he did what was wrong. The narrative tells us he respected the Baptist, because "he was a just man and an holy, and observed him; and when he heard him, he did many things, and heard him gladly*." This seems a hopeful account of Herod, but we know how it all ended. He was ready to do many things, except indeed to give up his cherished sin; he was entangled with Herodias, and had fallen under her dominion, and though he had a great respect for the Baptist, and was uneasy and afraid under his warnings, he could not make up his mind to free himself and act as his conscience, roused by John, told him that he ought. Lamentable example, illustrated by the experience

* Mark vi. 20.

of thousands who have listened to the seductions of this class of sins! How well is their effect described by Solomon:—"With her much fair speech she caused him to yield, with the flattering of her lips she forced him. He goeth after her straightway, as an ox goeth to the slaughter, or as a fool to the correction of the stocks; till a dart strike through his liver; as a bird hasteth to the snare, and knoweth not that it is for his life. Hearken unto me now therefore, O ye children, and attend to the words of my mouth. Let not thine heart decline to her ways, go not astray in her paths. For she hath cast down many wounded: yea, many strong men have been slain by her. Her house is the way to hell, going down to the chambers of death [b]." As is always the case, trifling with conscience he now became worse instead of better. Nothing can be more despicable than the picture of his weakness, working on which this bad woman and her daughter persuaded him to slay the man whom he revered as good and holy, who had found the way to touch his conscience, whom he dared not look in the face unmoved, but whom he sent an executioner to deal with secretly in the prison.

Oh wretchedness of weak bad men! What avail their good impressions, their good resolutions, or even their good deeds. "He heard him, and did many things," but it all ended in the murder of him whom God had sent to be His good angel. What a lesson for the worldly! Half measures

[b] Prov. vii. 21—27.

will not avail—half repentance, half amendment. After all the seeming good which John had wrought in him, the last state of this wretched man was worse than the first. No wonder that he could not forget what he had done; no wonder that his natural conscience was sensitively uneasy; no wonder that, as it has been with so many other sinners, he was tortured not only by pangs of self-condemnation, but by some strange superstitious dread. John's disciples had come with pious care, and taken the mangled trunk and laid it in a tomb; but Herod's conscience whispered that the blood so unrighteously poured forth called to Heaven against him, and that the tomb could not restrain the murdered prophet's power of vengeance. We read in the text, when afterwards he heard of Jesus, and the great things He did, and all were speculating who it could be who wielded so great a heavenly power, Herod said, "It is John, whom I beheaded: he is risen from the dead."

It fared badly with Herod in worldly matters from this time forward, and his misfortunes had a direct connexion with his sin. His story is given in all text-books.—How the father of his first wife, whom he had deserted for Herodias, eager to avenge the insult offered to his daughter, attacked him and totally destroyed his army; how he was for a time rescued from ruin by the interposition of the Emperor, but afterwards, when new difficulties stood in his way, went to Rome, where court favour soon turned against him, so that both he and Herodias were banished to the distant West, where he died unhonoured. No doubt uprightness is the best policy, even in this life; and though it is but probable that Herod's conscience, drugged by indulgence, soon ceased to rebuke him for the sinfulness of what he had done, no doubt he often thought bitterly of its folly, and allowed to himself, and complained we may believe reproachfully to Herodias, that the one notorious false step of his life had been his unlawfully and wickedly persisting in her society in spite of all the Baptist's warnings. Truly those who live recklessly in the world find before life is over that they have very many causes of bitter self-reproach even if they can drug and stupify their consciences.

My friends, how many an old man, now soured in spirit, is taking himself to task with bitter but unavailing reproaches for a youth misspent, for evil habits or dangerous friendships contracted in college days, which have hung like a chain around him, and ever prevented his rising, as his talents and opportunities might fairly have entitled him to expect. For one who extricates himself from such meshes hundreds plunge on for ever hopelessly involved. Be wise while it is time. Flee the early contagion and the early bondage. Even in this world it will be better. Who can tell how much better when we come to the inevitable death-bed?

But to return. Conscience, we have said, has two offices. We read* that the Holy Spirit convinces

* John xvi. 8.

men of sin, of righteousness, and of judgment. The natural conscience in its degree also works this threefold conviction;—it lets men know what is wrong, convincing them of sin; and what is right, convincing them of righteousness; and if they follow what is wrong it stirs within them some uneasy forebodings that they must one day suffer, thus convincing them of judgment. The first and the last of these offices of the natural conscience may be classed together: they have at least an intimate connexion. The same uneasy feeling which reminds a man of his sin whispers to him that judgment will follow, and indeed by the very pain it inflicts is a foretaste of that judgment. Conviction of sin and of judgment, then, are closely allied. Nay, if, as we know it has been urged, the most real terrors of the day of judgment are to spring from the memory being preternaturally stirred suddenly to remember and clearly see every particular of every sin of the whole life, however long it may have lain buried in forgetfulness, no doubt the sharp pangs which such stirring of the memory must inflict would be a fiery trial. Like that strange phenomenon told us by men who have been rescued from drowning, who say that when sensation ceases and death is imminent the soul in a dreamlike state wanders back, in a few seconds perhaps through many years, and sees familiar faces and hears voices long since forgotten, so it may be (for all we know) with death in every form; for no one comes back from a deathbed and tells us what are the soul's experiences in the act of dying. Certainly in many cases of sickness which are apparently leading to death, the memory is strangely stirred, and the spectres of old forgotten sins come back to gibe at us, when we had hoped they were laid for ever. All know how even at other times of no intense excitement, unexpectedly and inexplicably, as it were by accident, some strange association of sight or sound will recall a bitter memory, and a pang will pierce the heart, which not only reminds us of sin but punishes us for its commission. Bad men, I suppose, the worse they become, are less and less troubled with any such uneasy feelings, till it comes to the last. Then, indeed, there is reason to believe that the drugged conscience awakes from its torpor, and the poignant recollection of wicked deeds, at last seen to have been as foolish as they are wicked, becomes itself a hell.

God has given to us, then, the natural conscience, (I say not here how dependent, like every other faculty of mind or body, on favourable circumstances conducing to its development,)—but God has given us the natural conscience to make wickedness have its pain, its secret pain in itself, quite irrespective of any superadded penal consequences. God intends this natural conscience to be a help at first, warning us against sin; and though we may trifle with it, and send it to sleep, and think that it is dead, it will awake at last—either when we are dying or, more usually, after death—and vindicate its right as the commissioned voice of God within us, to cause His sentence against wickedness to ring in our ears, repeating ever in sounds which no obtuseness can mistake, 'Be sure, O sinner, that thy sin will find thee, has found thee out.'

Now if God has provided this natural protest against sin by the ordinary laws of conscience to be a help to all men,—all men, I mean, who are not idiots or sunk in some unnaturally degraded, savage state,—if God, I say, has provided this natural protest against sin, so when, through His great mercy in the Lord Jesus Christ, He sent the Holy Spirit to give us supernatural help, He ordained that the Spirit, convincing us of sin, should work, as it were, through the natural organs. The Christian conscience, enlightened, quickened by the Holy Ghost, is the conscience still; and the voice of God within Christians, speaking supernaturally, preserves the analogy of its natural utterances and effects. Let no man, then, think lightly of the natural conscience, disparaging it because of grace, for grace acts through it. Indeed, this seems to be a characteristic of all the operations of the Holy Spirit, that they are not manifested in some way unknown till the day of Pentecost, or never heard of at best beyond the circle of God's chosen people. Rather the Holy Spirit of God, in all His developments, works through natural organs, natural faculties, natural affections. He uses while He quickens, exalts, and purifies them. Read in the 12th chapter of the First Epistle to the Corinthians the list of the spiritual gifts: are they not all heavenly manifestations of powers which in some low imperfect way could be exercised, often with much difficulty, and weakness, and many efforts, and after all most imperfectly, but still which could be exercised in some sort of way by man naturally? Natural eloquence or the utterances of natural wisdom transformed by the fire from off the altar touching the lips with prophetic power; gifts of healing taking the place of the slow processes of the physician's art; natural longings and natural amiable feelings elevated into Christian graces of faith and love. And so when the Holy Spirit wakens the Divine voice within the soul, to guard it against sin, He speaks through the natural conscience, and does its work, but with a constraining force and efficacy which tells of a Divine power directly intervening. The Christian conscience in its office as convincing of sin, is then like the natural conscience, but it is a far more real protest, a protest more direct from God—it makes itself heard with His Almighty power.

True that there is a sort of intermediate state of the conscience, between the natural and the fully enlightened. The natural conscience in some men, from the very condition of their birth, is very nearly akin to the Christian conscience. The blessing of Christian parents descends in this respect on their children. It is at once the privilege and the trial of those who have received an early Christian training, that they cannot, for some years at least, shut their ears to the echoes of the Divine voice. They will succeed at last to their ruin if they persevere in resistance: but it is long before God gives them up, and while His warning is urgent to be heard they suffer at times very severely. Voices heard in childhood—home scenes—a mother's or a sister's love—how graciously are all softer feelings of our common humanity used by God in His dealings with the children of Christians, that He may check the excesses of thoughtless youth, while, in spite of natural conscience, it is hurrying to reckless and hopeless manhood. Let parents take courage to persevere in all efforts for the Christian training of their children, when they think of the power God thus gives to His appeals. A young man brought up in a Christian home cannot be happy in sin; and this is something. Truly the uneasiness will in time wear away, and the upbraiding memories cease to vex him, if he doggedly resists: but happy he whom they compel to listen, — in whom they work conviction, and at last stedfast repentance,—so that this weak, natural, half-Christian conscience becomes wholly Christian.

Then blessed be God in Jesus Christ, it does not, like the natural conscience, speak of judgment only, but of judgment and mercy united in Jesus Christ. The enlightened Christian conscience is very sensitive as to sins committed; it pains us and grieves us with the memory of them; it points to the coming judgment as a proof of sin's heinousness; but then it points also to that merciful arrangement whereby the Saviour is the judge, and tells the wounded heart where, in Him, to find the balm of forgiveness.

A few words will set forth this work of the Spirit. May it be traceable in our own hearts and lives, and may our feelings as to sin be such as God the Holy Spirit calls up through the Christian conscience! A man then, say, has been brought up (as all of us have) more or less as a Christian; baptized in infancy, instructed in childhood, no novice as he passes from boyhood into manhood as to what God commands and Christ has done, and the helps afforded to a Christian life. But then, perhaps, the whole matter has been to him a sort of formality, words by rote. It is curious to read in the old philosopher how people in his day repeated, without any real thought of their meaning, the maxims of the poets, just as Christians now have texts and extracts from formularies interwoven in their ordinary discourse, but have other maxims in their hearts. Ushered into life in the world—or into that dangerous lesser world which is so full of temptations here—in this frame of mind, with strong passions and weak convictions, according to his peculiar temperament the man either falls into notorious sin, or seeking as his heaven those objects which are best obtained by worldly respectability, exercises a worldly self-control, and grows up a respectable man, however irreligious. Where is the conscience in such a man? It is wonderful how in the world, and even here, a man may preserve his self-respect and the good opinion of others in spite of grievous sins. The very society he lives in being respectable, the very training and restraints to which he is subjected being more or less Christian, tends to quiet and deaden conscience. No doubt, as the months pass, openly or secretly he does many things of which conscience ought to be ashamed, but it is sleeping. What is the one thing we desire for such a man if he is to have spiritual life? That God would startle him, though it be by some sharp judgment; that the Holy Ghost, taking his conscience fully into His own keeping, would make it sensitive, would make it understand that many things are sins which before it thought lightly of; that thus convincing him of sin, the Spirit of God may shake him out of his easy, careless life, make him see the purity of God and the sinfulness of man in their true antagonism; and thus leading him to be disquieted and to distrust himself, may bring him to the Saviour for pardon and strength.

There is nothing more needful for every one of us than that we may see sin, all sin, and especially the sin we most cherish, in its true colours; dislike it; feel uneasy from the thought of its power over us; strive to be free from it; and thus turn in prayer and with good resolutions to Him who alone can make us free. To convince us of sin is the Holy Spirit's office. O Lord, send us Thy Holy Spirit thus to work in us!

And thus convinced of our sin, how are we saved from despair? Here, I repeat, is one great difference between the natural and the enlightened

Christian conscience. The natural conscience the more active it becomes renders us the more desperate; the Christian conscience does not convince us of sin without leading us to the sinner's Friend. Herod's conscience was like that of Judas. Both these men thought of their sin. The one appears, notwithstanding all his alarms, to have succeeded in silencing conscience through life; but despair came at last. The other could not silence it even for a few days, and so in despair before the week was ended he had hanged himself. But the Christian conscience has its likeness in David. The Psalmist, overwhelmed by his guilt, bitterly lamented it day by day, as his Psalms prove; he confessed his sin, and God put it away from him. And Peter, within an hour of his fall, was weeping bitterly, not from the motive of mere human shame when the Lord's eye was turned on him, but because he had scarcely committed his sin before he abhorred it. As soon as an opportunity offered, he was amongst the very first to hurry to his Saviour.

O Lord, convince us of sin; but may the conviction work in us a stedfast desire to keep near to the Lord Jesus Christ, the sinner's Friend!

SERMON VIII.

The Spirit interceding.

BY

J. R. WOODFORD, M.A.,
VICAR OF KEMPSFORD.

The Spirit interceding.

ROMANS viii. 27.

"Because He maketh intercession for the saints according to the will of God."

IT is worth while, when we are constrained by what is passing around us, to review all the foundations upon which our faith rests, to walk about Sion and go round about her, telling the towers thereof, to observe in how remarkable a degree the fundamental revelations of Scripture account for some of the most remarkable dispensations of God's Providence, and the most subtle phenomena of our moral being.

For example,—what a marvellous mixture of light and darkness, nobility and meanness, ignorance and knowledge, is the soul of man. How strangely are our vices the distortion of good rather than independent creations of evil. Take the lust of power. It has given birth to the foulest crimes, it has made the earth a desolation; yet ambition has in it, we instinctively feel, an element of greatness. Take again the desire of reputation. It can shew itself in the most childish exhibition of eccentricities. Yet to wish to live in the hearts and on the lips of mankind, who, while thoroughly aware of what unprincipled actions and unhallowed words this craving after honour has been the source, does not recognise in it a passion possessing much of that which is divine? And the Scripture doctrine of an original creation in uprightness, and a subsequent fall, furnishes at once the key which unlocks these secrets of our moral being? The lust of dominion,—what is this but the form which the lordship over creation assigned to the first man, assumes in a spoiled and disorganized being? The sense of shame, even its falsest application,—what is it but the relic of that high nature which was fashioned for ineffable communion with the Lord God Himself?

So, once more, when we look inwards, we discern the operation in our souls of three distinct powers. There is an influence dark, subtle, unwearied, ever leading us to make the lower passions of our nature the rule of action; and there is a contrary influence, whispering to us of a better way, of loftier destinies, of a truer happiness; of the glory and the bliss of a victory over self; and above these contending forces, holding the balance between them, the sole arbiter of the contest sits enthroned in mysterious sovereignty, the Will of the individual Man.

And, again, we say, how exactly does the Scripture teaching correspond with our personal experience. No better explanation, none which so commends itself to the general conscience of humanity, has ever been offered of the perpetual strife between truth and error, light and darkness in man, than that which the Bible gives of the source of the eternal war, the agency of a good Spirit in whom all that is holy is gathered up, and of an evil spirit in whom all evil is concentrated; and, co-existing with these, the thorough freedom of the human will.

It is on the work of one of these Powers that we have to fix our thoughts to-night. We are to speak of the "Spirit interceding." It is a subject which will lead us to touch upon some of the profoundest sensibilities of the soul of man: but here too will be found what we have mentioned by way of introduction—the thorough accordance of the doctrines of Revelation with the instincts and cravings of our own moral nature. St. Paul, in the eighth chapter of his Epistle to the Romans, alludes to many of the operations of the Holy Ghost. He describes Him as the Spirit of adoption, as the Spirit which witnesses conjointly with the human spirit as to our religious state, as the Helper of our infirmities. And then he passes on to another work of the same Divine agent, a work which at first sight does not seem so properly to be assigned to Him as to the second Person in the Trinity, "the Spirit itself maketh intercession for us." And in the text "He maketh intercession for the saints according to the will of God."

We have to examine into the nature, object, and manner of the intercession of God the Holy Spirit.

I. And first let us consider what the intercession of the Spirit is not.

(*a.*) Now, the great difficulty which hangs about the whole subject relates to the Person of the blessed Trinity, to whom the intercessory act is ascribed by the Apostle. We are accustomed to speak of Christ as our Mediator and Intercessor. "He," it is said, "ever liveth to make intercession for us." Again, "It is Christ that died, yea rather that is risen again, Who is even at the right hand of God, Who also maketh intercession for us." And so distinctly and pre-eminently is this His work, that it was repeatedly prefigured in the ancient dispensation. The intercession of the Spirit must not then be understood in any such way as would trench upon the office of Christ as our eternal High Priest and Intercessor. There is, indeed, perfect unity of action between the second and third Persons in the Trinity. The Holy Ghost dwells within us as the Spirit of Christ. So complete is the unity that it is written of Christ, "The Lord is that Spirit." Yet He is ever described as a distinct independent Agent. All His offices have a direct relation to Christ, but they are never confounded with those of Christ. "He," says our Lord, "shall receive of Mine." "He shall bring all things to your remembrance, whatsoever I have said. Whatsoever He shall hear, that shall He speak." All these passages indicate distinct action. And so of intercession. The Intercession of Christ is, if we may so say, a local work, carried on in one spot; viz. the highest Heaven. It consists (1) in the receiving the prayers of men below, and wafting them onward to the

Father. Hence the force of that cry in the *Gloria in Excelsis*, "Thou that takest away the sins of the world, receive our prayer,"—as though He, our Aaron, must first take into His hands the offering of worship which is to be laid before the mercy-seat. It consists (2) in a perpetual pleading for us before the Throne His own death and Passion. Therefore did He convey into Heaven His own human Body, bearing still the marks of the nails, and the spear, that in the house not made with hands there might be continued, as in the earthly temple, a perpetual remembrance of His death. Thus, as our Intercessor, Christ not only receives our petitions, so that aspirations in themselves too feeble to enter into God's ear, are reiterated by Him, and gifted with an irresistible force by His advocacy, but that as He prayed for His disciples on earth so still in heaven, by His wounded though glorified Body, He urges the cause of His people. Now, the intercession of the Holy Spirit is distinct from this. There seem to be two great characteristics of the work of the Holy Ghost in the Church; the first, that it is subjective rather than objective, the second, that its scene is not heaven but earth. Christ departed from the earth in order that the Spirit might descend and abide with us; communicating unto and impressing upon the soul, to its renewal and sanctification, that which Christ had wrought. We look accordingly for the intercession of the Spirit not in the Holy of Holies above, not in the depths of the light inaccessible, not amid the burning ranks of angels and archangels, but here, in the tabernacle of the human soul, amid the cloud and darkness of a half-illumined nature, amongst the infirmities and errors of a marred and shattered creation.

(*b.*) But further, the intercession of the Divine Spirit may not be confounded with the praying of the human spirit. To consider His prayers for the saints, which St. Paul dwells on, as the same thing as their prayers for themselves, as though the pleading of the Spirit for men were only a theological way of expressing men's pleadings for themselves, would be to take away all force from the Apostle's language. It may indeed be very difficult when we have determined the place of the Spirit's intercessions to be in the soul of man, to draw the line clear between His action and the soul's action. But this is only one example of that great difficulty which meets us at every step of our search into the things of God, the difficulty of separating the divine and human element where both co-exist. See how this runs through every Christian mystery. The union of the two Natures in the Person of Christ,— how impossible is it for us to reconcile and explain the action of each nature, whole and perfect as we believe it to be; to describe how He, who knew all things, could grow in knowledge; how He, who was one with the Father, could continue all night in prayer to the Father; how He, to whom the future was as the present, could hope or fear. In the life of our Blessed Lord the twofold elements of

His mysterious personality are continually coming up, defying our reason to lay bare this secret of the Lord.

It is the same with the doctrine of Sacraments. Here, too, there is a union of the divine and human, the natural and the spiritual. Yet the manner of the union distances all the strivings of our intellect to sift and define. And is it not precisely the same difficulty which besets us in regard to the question of inspiration? The work of the Spirit and the work of man in the compilation of Scripture; where the influence of the Divine agent ends and that of the human begins; the way in which the one operated upon the other—all these are but the transfer to the subject of inspiration of the self-same inexplicable questions which exercised the mind of the Church in earlier times with reference to the Incarnation of Christ and Sacramental grace.

And we must be prepared, therefore, for similar difficulties, when we have to deal with the conjoint work of the Spirit of God and the spirit of man. That the natural conscience is quickened and enlightened by the Holy Ghost may be readily conceived; but it is hard to penetrate further into that deep where He worketh, so as to separate the steps of that united operation. Similarly with the Intercession of the Spirit. It is within the temple of the soul that this ineffable pleading of the Holy One is carried on. It is a cry out of the human heart, from Him that sitteth co-equal with the Father and the Son upon the throne; a cry from the Eternal Life-giver; a real Intercession for the saints; by no means to be explained away as though it were the same thing as the natural utterance of the human soul. Distinct in origin, although blending (He alone knoweth how) with the voice of the creature; the one heavenly, the other of the earth; the one human, the other divine; the interceding of the Spirit is no mere poetical expression to denote the sinner's own prayers for himself, but a true and proper utterance of the Holy One.

We exclude, therefore, from the notion of the Spirit interceding any such solemn interpellation and exposition of human need before the Everlasting Throne such as forms the special work of Christ Jesus. We exclude also such a conception of it as would deprive it of all reality. How in the depths of our moral being, amid the broken fragments of that once sinless sanctuary, the Lord of Life and the soul unite in the uplifting of one voice of supplication, belongeth to those hidden things which we may never fathom; nevertheless, we are not to be deterred in this, any more than in other subjects, by the confessed difficulty of harmonizing the human and the divine, from putting aside any explanation which would not leave it a vital reality, the intercession of the Spirit for the saints according to the will of God.

II. But now we pass on to consider the positive side of the question. What is that intercession wherewith the Spirit of God intercedeth for us out of the ark of our own souls, yet with a real and personal action of His own? There is a parallel passage referring to the defence which the Apostles would have to make from time to time, which may help us at this point. "When they shall deliver you up, take no thought how or what ye shall speak; for it shall be given you in that same hour what ye shall speak. For it is not ye that speak, but the Spirit of your Father which speaketh in you." We are not to understand the passage as though our Lord encouraged them to be careless and idle in preparing themselves for giving an answer as to the hope that was in them; He does not exhort them to take no pains about their own defence; but only not to be over-disturbed and anxious as to their qualifications for the task, just as on another occasion he warns them not to be over-careful about to-morrow. He does not mean that there should be given them instantaneously such a degree of supernatural aid as would render useless all previous human diligence; but that they were to prepare themselves calmly and collectedly for the great controversy with Heathen and Jew, believing that in the hour of trial One would be on their side whom their enemies knew not, prompting their thoughts, and elevating their intellect, and lending power to their speech: and this so completely that their words would be transformed in their passage from their lips into the words of One mightier than they. And exactly as the Eternal Spirit co-operated with the Apostles when called on for their defence before rulers and kings, does He act with our hearts in the preparation and outpouring of that full and earnest prayer which finds its way upward into God's ears. The faint and ignorant cry of the human soul, dead in trespasses and sins, desiring to pray, yet, like the disciples, requiring to be taught, He, the indwelling Spirit, knowing far better than we know our wants, knowing also the very mind of God, adopts, and purifies, and deepens; our imperfect petitions are transfigured by His power so as to become as much His as ours. They reach not heaven as they leave our hearts, but as they are quickened and rendered complete by Him.

There are two ways in which the Divine Spirit thus deals with our prayers, so marvellously changing them as that they become His own.

(*a.*) First, He corrects what is amiss in the breathings of the soul in which He dwells. Theologians have stated a variety of ways in which a sincere Christian, a saint as St. Paul calls him in the text, may unwittingly err in his prayers:—if he desires any temporal good which may be injurious to his spiritual welfare; if, on the other hand, he prays as the Apostle prayed, to be rid of any thorn in the flesh, any bodily infirmity which is really essential to his soul's health; if he covets any high grace out of mere worldly emulation, as the sons of Zebedee besought a true honour but from an unworthy motive; if he craves what is wrong from a sincere but mistaken zeal; if he beseeches the immediate gift of what would be more profitably deferred; if he seeks any condition of life unsuited to his peculiar character. Now these, you will observe, are all defects which may pertain to the prayers of an honest and loyal heart. And what is the action of the Holy Ghost upon them? Why, that He, residing in, and acting with, the regenerate soul, knowing our necessities before we ask, and our ignorance in asking, illumines the soul as to what its want is, or pleads for that true need which lies at the root of every prayer, so that under His gracious influence our prayers are accepted as the desire of our hearts, not for the false good which we have ignorantly implored, but for the real good which we know not. The human spirit asks for silver, and the Divine Intercessor pleads that the prayer be answered with gold. This is the meaning of that clause in the collect of St. Chrysostom, the infinite wisdom of which so few appreciate,—" Fulfil now, O Lord, the desires and petitions of Thy servants as may be most expedient for them;" not according to the outward expression of our lips, but according to the deeper, truer meaning of the Holy Ghost that dwelleth in us; that Spirit which, as He prompteth us to pray at all, so doth He transform the prayers of the saints that they become His own; and in the erring utterances of finite knowledge is heard the unerring voice of the Eternal Spirit, uplifted for the real welfare of him who prays."

(*b*.) Nor is this all. "The Spirit itself," says the Apostle, "intercedeth for us with groanings which cannot be uttered." The verse follows a wonderful description of the whole creation groaning and travailing in pain together; as though all the disorders of the present system, the sufferings of animal life, the convulsions of the material universe, the earthquake that shatters, and the tempest that devastates, the pestilence that walketh in darkness, as they are the consequences of the fall, were also the birth-pangs through which is to be generated a nobler creation. "And we ourselves also, who have the first-fruits of the Spirit, groan within ourselves." If all around, animate and inanimate, bears the impress of an imperfect and transitory state; if it is manifestly at once the wreck of a holier life, and the embryo of a more glorious being, not less in the human soul are there ever-ringing voices, not of this earth, asserting an affinity with higher, vaster, mightier existences; ceaselessly pleading to be free from the weariness and disappointment of the present troubled condition; to shake off the mists which obscure our vision, the fetters that impede our progress, and to go forth into wider ranges of thought and knowledge than is at present permitted. All that dissatisfaction which attends the greatest worldly success; that weariness of living which sometimes falls like a cold shadow upon the path of those who have lived most honourably and usefully; all those speculations after truth, which at once so strangely fascinate and disturb the mind; the restless impatience of being bound down to follow in the wake of other men's thoughts; all that untiring effort to widen the horizon of the human mind and push further back the thick darkness which may be felt; the constant attempt to hurry into day more of the secrets of the universe, fulfilling again and again the words of Solomon,— "The eye is not satisfied with seeing, neither the ear with hearing;" what are all these but the groanings of the human soul after its true but undiscovered home, its proper but unknown life,— groanings which cannot be uttered, ineffable desires not to be clothed in speech, after an infinite but indescribable good?

And here, again, we may find a sphere for the action of the eternal interceding Spirit. It is His gracious work in the hearts of God's servants to direct aright to right objects and in a right channel these groanings of redeemed humanity; His work, to give form and substance to these profound but vague aspirations of the soul of man; to prevent men from lapsing into mere idle dreamers, instead of being energetic labourers in God's world, which is the great snare of intellectualism; to convert these undefined desires, groanings not to be put into words by human philosophy, into specific anxiety to be shewn God's will and enabled to do it, specific prayers for the mastery of passion, the purification of the appetites, the extermination of sin; for the being made earnest fellow-workers with God here in the dispersion of ignorance and the relief of suffering, for the being conformed now unto His likeness in all purity and truth, and thus prepared for a closer vision of Himself hereafter.

Surely here is intercession real as that carried on by Christ in the courts above; nor to be confounded with the faltering utterances of the human mind, lisping, childlike, of truths wholly beyond its ken, telling of wants and fears whose root lies deep in mysteries it dreams not of. Aye, and just as the well-taught man catches out of the mouth of babes and sucklings the unconscious enunciation of some sublime verity, so what God hears and answers from His holy place is not the indefinite yearnings of His servants, but in and through them the mighty pleading of His own indwelling Spirit, making intercession for them not according to their degree of knowledge, but according to His own perfect will concerning them.

Men and brethren, it is a very practical subject on which we have dwelt, a subject full at once of warning and encouragement. If it be certain that when we pray, out of our hearts prayeth the Spirit of God likewise, then what an unspeakable solemnity attaches to every act of devotion. Is it indeed so that when I kneel down to pray, the Everlasting Spirit waiteth to catch my soul's speech to adopt it for His own, and echo it on in a deeper, truer sense, and with more exceeding power? Then, assuredly, I can never venture to hurry over my prayers drowsily and thoughtlessly, seeing not I alone, but the Holy Ghost, prayeth with me, and that I am, as it were, to put words in His mouth.

And contrariwise, if He so intercedeth for me, then if I do strive to pray aright, to concentrate my thoughts and lift up my soul, although the weakness of my nature cause me ofttimes to ask feebly and to ask amiss, yet not in vain shall I have worshipped, because He, the Spirit, into my faltering accents will have thrown His strength, and through my blinded speech will have poured forth the prayer of His all-perfect knowledge.

SERMON IX.

The Spirit comforting.

BY

E. B. PUSEY, D.D.,

REGIUS PROFESSOR OF HEBREW, AND CANON OF CHRIST CHURCH.

The Spirit comforting.

ST. MATTHEW v. 4.

"Blessed are they that mourn: for they shall be comforted."

WE live in an awful world. Look which way we will, within us or without, on God's revelation of His holiness, or His unutterable condescension, the unspeakableness of His free infinite love, or His just condemnation of sin, the marvellous fertility of His ways in winning us to Himself, and the almost boundless prodigality of the riches of divine mercy, or that dreadful condition of His creature, which has made itself for ever incapable of His love,—our existence is an awful gift. The infinity of His condescension in our redemption, and the endless sufferings of those who have to the end shut out God, are in sad harmony together. It can have been for no light cause that God abhorred not the Virgin's womb, God was born, God, in the likeness of man, and having united that Man for ever with Himself, went about among us, partook of all our sinless infirmities; God (not the Godhead) suffered; God the Lord of glory was crucified[a]; God, not the

[a] 1 Cor. ii. 8.

Godhead, but He who "in the beginning was with God, and was God," died. To persevere in sin against such inventiveness of the love of God, what is it but "an Angel's hopeless fall [b]?" God has done more for us than for them. The mysteries of the redemption were wrought for man, not for the devil and his angels.

The Gospels are full of love, for they are full of the words and works of Jesus. Yet you can scarcely open a page of them, but your eye will fall upon words of awe; so false as well as deadlily delusive to the soul is that teaching which so dwells upon that infinite love of God as to blot out the thought of His awful holiness, and shut out from sinners the wholesome terror of hell, until they fall into it irremediably.

Even God's words of comfort shew the unreality of such pictures of this our being, in which God has entrusted us, His creatures, with that awful choice, upon which our eternity depends, freely to choose or to refuse for ever Himself, the All-Good. One special office, one title of God the Holy Ghost is, to be "the Comforter." Our Comforter is Almighty, is God. His Presence is an especial gift of our departing Lord to His Church, to ourselves. "I will pray the Father for you, and He shall give you another Comforter, that He may abide with you for ever; even the Spirit of Truth; whom the world cannot receive [c]." Another Comforter! An-

[b] Keble's Christian Year, Thirteenth Sunday after Trinity.
[c] St. John xiv. 16, 17.

other to replace Himself! and He, God proceeding from God, to abide with us and in us, if we will, for ever. But then what a condition of life does this open to us! An Almighty, ever-present, divine Comforter implies a continual, universal, unceasing need of comfort.

Comfort! The world hates the thought. For comfort implies sorrow, and the world would have none of it; or, at the most, it would have it only, when it cannot escape it, when sorrow does come; and even then, it would have as little as may be to do with supernatural comfort, or, alas! with the Comforter. Then, too, it would rather remove or displace its griefs with fresh cause of grief; fresh pleasures, again to pall; fresh joys, again to fade; fresh hopes, again to fail; fresh honours, ambitions, delights, vain-glories, to perish with this perishing world. As our Blessed Lord prophesied, so it is, —"Whom the world cannot receive, because it seeth Him not, neither knoweth Him." The world shrinketh from the Spirit of Truth, because it clings to its errors; it loathes the thought of the Comforter, because it would be all-sufficient to itself in its joys, and would know no sorrow.

But is then sorrow only for those afflictive visitations of God, by which He awakens men out of sin's death-sleep to themselves and to Him? Is there no abiding sorrow, no abiding consolation, no supernatural sorrow, and supernatural comfort? Our Lord does not speak of any passing feeling or quickly-fading grace, when He pronounces the blessedness of the poor in spirit, the merciful, the pure in heart, the a-hungered and athirst after righteousness. So neither is it a passing grace, much less is it mere natural sorrow over those causes of sorrow, with which God, in His love, mercifully besprinkles the absorbing pleasures of this life. Rather it is an abiding sorrow, sweeter than all life's sweetnesses; for it is a sorrow from God, unto God, according to God; a sorrow, the fruit of grace, the parent of joy, the condition of supernatural consolation. "Blessed are they that mourn: for they shall be comforted."

Is this our home? are we in Paradise? are we in that state, in which and for which God made us? are we in possession of our heavenly birth-right? are we at rest in ourselves? are we satisfied with our past or present? is our future secure? is our relation to God what we wish? True! we have consolations of nature, which, when pure, are earnests of the love of God. We may have unspeakable consolations of grace. But consolations, (as I said,) imply a need of consolation; they imply a sorrow of heart, which has to be comforted.

Our Lord's words are so large, that they must comprise all which is not "of the nature of sin." In itself, the word "mourn" almost always belongs to a tender sorrow. It is originally the mourning over the dead[d]; it is the inner feeling expressed by tears; it is sorrow over that which has been and is not. In this sense, too, "blessed are they

---

[d] The word is πενθεῖν.

that mourn;" and so we may well think that our Lord meant to include these too in His blessing, if the sorrow have but that condition, which is presupposed in any blessing from His mouth, that it be "a sorrow according to God[e]," in conformity with, subdued to, following the track of, His All-Holy Will. He who had known all earthly joy, and glory, and wisdom, and fame, first of His day, with whose wisdom none competed except to be vanquished, was chosen as the organ of revealing the blessedness of sorrow. "It is better to go to the house of mourning," [i.e. where they mourn the life just fled,] "than to go to the house of feasting: for that is the end of all men; and the living will lay it to his heart. Sorrow is better than laughter: for by the sadness of the countenance the heart is made better[f]." Blessed is a joy according to God, abounding in thanksgiving, bounding upward to its God, holding His gifts unvaryingly from Himself, delighting not only in them, but because they are choice gifts of its Father's Hand. But deeper far is a "sorrow according to God." For in joy we love God in, for, with, His gifts; in sorrow the gifts are gone, and we adore God mutely for His wisdom in withdrawing them, and love Him for Himself. Mourning drives a person into himself. It takes off the false glare of this showy treacherous world. It wakens up old memories, which he would wish buried for ever. It is a lightning flash on a precipice before his feet, and, below, the pit of

---

[e] 2 Cor. vii. 10. [f] Eccl. vii. 2, 3.

hell. It speaks of death, and of what is to be after death. It shews him to himself as a whole; how evil acts have become habits; how things in him, seemingly unconnected, are bound together by one unseen thread, and that thread sin, or of sin; how all or most of his good has been cankered by this secret unsuspected worm; how self has been, in all, his secret law, his lawgiver, his idol, his god. Blessed, then, is the outward condition of mourning, blessed far above all outward joy, which becomes, through repentance, the vestibule of heaven.

Yet piercing as is the unveiled sight of that resurrection of man's buried sins; crushing as is their accumulated number, as they exhibit themselves all at once to his gaze, (faint image of the Judgment Day, because our Lord's reproachful look is not there,) or as they throng in long procession, another, and another, and another, until the brain turns dizzy at the sight of self; shocking as it is to see what seemed good deeds look mere counterfeits, with which we would have bribed conscience and mocked God—be the sight a baptism of fire, there is a rainbow in the thick cloud, there is, in the sight, an earnest of God's mercy. God would not have shewn us the sight in this life, but that He willed us to repent, and to forgive us. "No interval separates the tears of the sinner and the mercy of the Saviour." God who said "Let there be light," and there was light, by the greater Omnipotence of His love, says of repented sin, Let it be as though it had never been; and forthwith, it is not, to condemnation; it exists only in memory, the safeguard of humility, the quickener of forgiven love. Yet not only so. Sorrow is evermore, through God, the parent of Divine joy. Whatever has been our course, whether preserved in Baptismal grace, and in the main ever looking heavenwards, or brought back to ourselves and to God by affliction, one is the experience of all, who are now in a state of grace and know themselves. "It is good for me that I have been in trouble, that I might learn Thy statutes;" "Thou in faithfulness hast afflicted me [g]."

Deep were those thoughts of one still young, who having thanked his God for all His marvellous love in childhood, boyhood, and in the bolder range of "reason's awful power," went on in words which once were here well-known familiar tones [h]:—

> "Yet, Lord, in memory's fondest place
>   I shrine those seasons sad,
> When, looking up, I saw Thy Face
>   In kind austereness clad.
>
> "I would not miss one sigh or tear,
>   Heart-pang or throbbing brow;
> Sweet was the chastisement severe,
>   And sweet its memory now.
>
> "Yes, let the fragrant scars abide,
>   Grace-tokens in Thy stead;
> Faint shadows of the spear-pierced Side
>   And thorn-encompassed Head."

And so it is unto the end. Not success, but checks; not praise, but dispraise; not gain, but

[g] Ps. cxix. 71—75.
[h] Lyra Apostolica, n°. 23; Chastisement, (Dr. Newman's).

loss; not this world's joy, but sorrow; are, to hoar hairs, God's choicest gifts, sorrow turning into joy, privation crowned by the riches of His consolation; the touch, from which the flesh shrinks, is the token of the presence of that Spirit of burning, which scorches to save.

"I would not part with one pang that I have had, no not for the whole world," were the almost parting words[1] of one, who had had high rank, wealth, political position, talent, brilliant wit, popularity, and a closing year of intensest bodily suffering.

Yet although these are part of a law of God, they do not work their effects by force of that law. Despair, not repentance, would be the natural fruit of chastisement; passionate, profitless grief would be the natural produce of deep loss; discontent the result of bodily suffering. Not of itself, but by the brooding of the Spirit over the troubled chaos, is it hushed into order and repose, and yieldeth life; only through the healing presence of the Comforter does "the sorrow of this world," which "worketh death," become "the sorrow according unto God," which "worketh the repentance unto salvation not to be repented of."

Yet neither the sorrow through which God brings back the dead soul to life, nor those other sorrows through which He quickens it anew to deeper, more inward life in Him, or burns out what might ex-

[1] The words were said to the late Bishop of Oxford, who told them to me.

haust, or weaken, or choke that life, can come up to the full meaning of our Lord's words. For then He would rather have said, "Blessed are they that have mourned," or, "that shall have mourned;" not, "the mourning," that is, "they who are ever mourning [k]."

This leads us to a deeper thought as to our Lord's words. For now we have two seeming contradictories, an abiding mourning and an abiding joy. We have joy, yea exceeding joy, an exulting, bounding joy [l], as a Christian duty,—a triumph [m] given to us by God in Christ; and Christ Himself pronounces us blessed, if we are ever mourners.

Plainly, then, the mourning must be something quite other than the world means by it. For mourning may have peace; nay, rather, true mourning will always have a deep still peace; but how should it have exuberance of joy?

---

[k] I find this in St. Gregory of Nyssa (De Beatitud., Or. iii. Opp., tom. i. p. 781) :—"The Word seemeth to me, in that prolonged action of mourning, to suggest something deeper than I have said, leading us on to conceive of something beside this. For if He had pointed only to repentance for transgression, it had suited better with this, if those had been pronounced blessed, who 'have mourned' (τοὺς πενθήσαντας), than those 'who are habitually mourning' (τοὺς εἰσαεὶ πενθοῦντας); as, to compare *their* condition who are in a diseased state, we pronounce those happy who have been cured, not those who are in a continual course of cure."

[l] ἀγαλλιᾶσθε, St. Matt. v. 12; ἀγαλλίασις, Acts ii. 46; ἀγαλλιᾶσθε χαρᾷ ἀνεκλαλήτῳ, 1 Pet. i. 8: add Acts xvi. 34, 1 Pet. i. 6, iv. 13.   [m] 2 Cor. ii. 14.

It has the joy all the more because it is habitual. Look at any deep loss of this earth, which has severed life in twain, because for the time it has severed those who were as one. Time flows by; the impassioned grief is mellowed; there comes a serene calm and reigns, and is the habitual state of the soul. But the survivor is not as before. Life is gilded from above; duty done to God, love to God, kindness and love to man, natural affections, bring a peaceful joy; yet, deep below, there is one unchanging feeling, such as that which, after years had passed, burst from the aged Patriarch's soul, "Joseph is not."

I said mourning (the word which our Lord uses) especially relates to sources of joy, which we have had and have not. What is it which the whole human race had and has lost? What is it, which we all more or less deeply lose, and which we never in this life can recover? Innocence was that great gift of God to man in Paradise, blameless life, unclouded intercourse with God. "What we now," says a Father [n], "conceive of only by imagining, all were shed around that first man, immortality and bliss, self-rule untyrannised, life without grief or care, passed in things divine, gazing on the All-good, with unveiled mind. Such were we. How then can we but mourn, contemplating our present wretchedness by the side of our then blessedness? What in us was lofty, lowered; what was in the image of the heavenly, inearthed; what was destined

---

[n] St. Greg. Nyss., l. c., pp. 785, 786.

to reign, enslaved; what was created for immortality, corrupted by death; what was passionless, exchanged for this passionate and perishing life; our unenslaved freewill now lorded over by ills so many and so great, that we cannot easily count the tyrants over us! For each of the passions in us, when it gains the mastery, becomes the lord over its slave, and, like a tyrant, seizing the citadel of the soul, afflicts our subjected nature by the things subdued to him, using at his will our thoughts as his servants. So are anger, cowardice, rashness, our passions pleasurable or painful, hatred, strife, mercilessness, harshness, envy, flattery, memory of injuries and unfeelingness, and all the contrary passions, so many tyrants and masters, enslaving the soul, as a prisoner of war, each to his own dominion."

A storm without might be with great peace within. Strife is afflictive, but leaves, by God's grace, no sting or stain of sin. Few and fleet are our pilgrim-years here; and God has engoldened our transient dwelling-place with multiplied radiancy of His love. Not the strife, but the defeat; not even our want of self-mastery, as such, but our own free evil choice, is life's deep sorrow. The embitterment of life is sin against the infinite love of our all-good God.

The bitterness is sweetened by forgiveness; the gentle, still, deep, sorrow remains; the deeper, because the more still. Think of one deeply loved who, under whatever temptation, had been guilty of the blackest ingratitude to father, husband, friend; (it is the very picture of us in the Prophet, " Go love a woman, loved of a husband (himself) yet an adulteress, according to the love of the Lord to the children of Israel, who look to other gods°;") could the forgiven ever cease to mourn? would not the exceeding tenderness of forgiving, unreproaching, love, draw forth the deeper sorrow?

What were all created love, gathered and concentrated into one, compared with the love of God for each of us? I would not say, it were nothing. Very beautiful is pure, created, love, because it is His highest creation, the image of His Being, Who is Love. But all conceivable love, which God has created, or shall create, or could, if He so willed, ever create, were but finite; and His love to each one of us is infinite. And against this infinite love we have sinned. Each act of wilful sin casts back upon God this His infinite love, compares His creature with Himself, and tells God to His face, " I choose this pleasure, this pride, this vanity, this lie, this misery, rather than Thee, and Thine infinite love." What, when such sins have been accumulated? What, when years of life have been spent in such preference of self, self-will, ambition, vilenesses, to God? What, when at best almost all life is one ingratitude, since at best all love which we return for that infinite love is so poor, so mean, so self-seeking, that people would be ashamed to offer it all to any good creature of His whom they deeply loved!

° Hos. iii. 1; see Comm. p. 23.

And all this, on repentance for love of Himself, God has forgiven, blots out, ignores, reproaches not. "God is a God of the present." He accepts the disobedient penitent son, who told Him to His face, "I go not," yet goes at last, as if he had, from the first, done His will. Should we not have hearts of stone if this untiring, despised, provoked, overcoming, and then unreproaching love of God, did not melt us? And can we then enjoy the manifold, daily, ever-varying goodness of our God, and not mourn that we ever sinned against it?

This mourning is not sad, or dejected, or downcast. It casts no cloud over the brightest cheerfulness which God spreads over life. Rather, it is the supernatural source of comfort above nature. For He who gives the sorrow gives also the joy. In all eternity redeemed man cannot forget what he has been. His own special blessedness would be less, if he could. For our bliss will be, by God's mercy, in the infinite love of our God; and we should know less of that infinite love, if we did not know how much He had forgiven us, how His victorious love had won us to Himself. St. Peter's bliss would be less, if he could forget that look which won him back to himself and to his Lord. St. Mary Magdalene would be less blessed in her Lord's love, if she could forget His love, when she washed His feet with her tears. The robber would not, if he could, be deprived of the memory of his Lord's love, which pardoned that his last blasphemy on the cross, accepted the confession which it had given, and admitted him alone of His redeemed to His side in Paradise.

But since the memory of forgiven sin will intensify the joy of heaven, so penetrated will it be and transfigured with Divine love, then neither, by the grace of God, will it cast any shadow over life's pure joys here. Nay rather, there is no true joy without it. True joy can never be in partial ignorance, or in looking away from oneselves. The self we would flee from, meets us unbidden; any chance word, any old remembrance, awakens it. Some word of God suggests it. We are in doubt and must have misgiving about ourselves; and that misgiving relates to eternity and our eternal doom! God will not, in His mercy, let us rest, where rest is disease or death. There is no health, until the last drop of bad blood has been squeezed out or transmuted by His grace. Our only joy can be, not in ourselves, but in God; not in ignorance that we are sinners, or how deep our sins, but in pouring out all our sins at the feet of Jesus and in His forgiveness. And then man's true joy is in thankfulness to God, and to Jesus God Man, for atoning, pardoning love. So God transmutes our poverty into the riches of His grace; our short-comings into the overflow of His love; our badness into the occasions of His goodness; our hateful memories of what is hateful, sin, into channels of His purifying grace, the joy of redeemed love.

Our humility, repentance, hatred for sin, meekness and tenderness to our fellow-sinners, safety against relapse, thankfulness to God, growth in grace, all are involved in the vivid memory that we are forgiven sinners. Blessed, then, is the mourning, in itself, which is the guardian of our restored grace, which makes us of one mind with God, hating what He hates, and tender with His tenderness, compassionate towards our fellow-servants, even as He had pity on us.

But through the exuberance of His love, the bitter waters are turned into sweetness by the wood of His Cross. *They shall be comforted.* Comfort is not the mere negation, or absence of sorrow. It is not, (as men's comfort is,) a powerless sympathy, soothing, in a measure, for the love which there is in it, but not reaching to the depths of the wound below. God's comfort, as "His Word," "is with power[p]." The comfort is from the Almighty Comforter, who comforts, not in word but in deed. It were little in comparison, had He said, that their mourning should be ended, that their tears should be wiped away. He says much more, "They shall be comforted." Their comfort is not, then, from within, but from without; it is an action upon the soul, and that from God, who vouchsafes to take, as one of His titles, "the Father of mercies," (mercies as manifold as our needs,) "and the God of all comfort[q]."

We have then an abiding, supernatural comfort from an Almighty Comforter. Mourning and comfort meet together; "deep crieth unto deep," the

[p] Ps. xxix. 4; St. Luke iv. 32.   [q] 2 Cor. i. 3.

depth of man's misery to the depth of God's mercy. Wherever the cry of the soul is, *there* is the ear of God. "Thou preparest the heart; Thine ear hearkeneth thereto [r]."

It bespeaks, as I said, one universal troubled state of man's being, that God the Holy Ghost should have that title and office towards us, the Comforter. Yet this being so, what is in itself evil is, by the touch of God, transformed into a superabundance of good. "Where sin abounded, there the grace superabounded [s]." Where sorrow comes, there is a proportioned superabundance of consolation.

But consolation were as nothing without the Consoler. What man needs is God. Natural joy cannot content the heart, which was made for God. Nothing can content it, except what is from God and to God. *The* joy of consolation is that it is the touch of God. "They shall be comforted" by the Comforter, a continual action of God on the soul meeting the soul's continual desire.

And so that last treasure of man's innocence, for which he mourns, the intercourse with God, is, by his mourning, restored to him. Not that consolation, or any spiritual sweetness, must be our end. Nothing in ourselves must be our end, but God only. Our end is, by God's grace, to become holier, less unlike God, less ungrateful to Him for His forgiving love. Our sorrow must not take its eyes off from God. We wish, if we could, to make

[r] Ps. x. 17.   [s] ὑπερεπερίσσευσεν, Rom. v. 20.

amends to Him; we cannot tell Him often enough to satisfy ourselves, "Would, O God, for love of Thee, I had never, never, displeased Thee!" We know that we cannot change the past, whatever it has been; but we can oppose a strong contrary will to that will, wherewith we offended God; and speaking thus to God strengthens our will and longing, as speaking to man, except in the view of God, weakens it. For God looks on the soul which He has led by His grace to look up to Him; He strengthens the soul, which looks to Him, its strength. Every such longing of the soul is a portion of the unutterable groanings of the Spirit[1], whereby He suggests desires mightier than words can utter, more than the heart knows how to contain; "Would that I had ever loved Thee!" And what the Spirit suggests within is heard on high; for it is the voice of God, which means more than our thoughts can grasp, pleading with God, by virtue of *His* merits Who, being God, for us sinners became man.

This is the special value of the deep penitential character of the prayers of our Church. This is why we, instinctively, love the Litany; why, before the Communion, the deeper confession after the Commandments, and that in which we own "the burden of our sins intolerable," suit our heart so well. It is in the presence of the deepest love that the sense of forgiven sin is deepest. The penitence which suits Lent, in another way suits Easter or

[1] Rom. viii. 27.

Pentecost, or the reception of our Lord's Body and Blood. The sorrow of forgiven love is a festival joy; for we sorrow, because we have been, are, so unworthy of that infinite love, wherewith God hath loved us, wherewith He loveth us.

God grant, my sons, that ye may have no deeper cause for sorrow than ye now have, that ye may not need that mighty burst of sorrow, wherewith a soul is restored from death. Yet there must be, I fear, among you some, whom deadly sin crept over, in years yet earlier than yours even now are, less deadly then, because you knew not its whole deadliness. One cannot but have fears, when the body is so much pampered, the "keeping under," which an Apostle thought needful to himself, so despised. Abuse not what I have said, as though ye might have the pleasure of sin now, the joy of forgiven sinners hereafter. To sin, in hope of God's forgiveness hereafter, is one of the forerunners of the sin for which there is no forgiveness, because there is no repentance. Your Saviour, who hath revealed Himself to you, looketh to "see" in you "of the travail of His soul," and to be "satisfied." God the Father, who loved you in all eternity, and who made you in and for His infinite love, looketh and waiteth, that ye should answer the end for which He made you. God the Holy Ghost, by whose agency, ere you knew good or evil, ye were severed from the world, and who made you sons of God and members of Christ, who has ever put every good thought into you, who now perhaps is reminding you of your high nobility and suggesting to you to live worthily of your birth of God, waiteth to give you all the treasures of His grace, love, joy, peace, the unutterableness of His consolations. Defraud not God of yourselves. Defraud not yourselves of God. Give to God that which is His, His image, the price of the Blood of God, yourselves. Say to God, "I am Thine. Would, for love of Thee, I had ever lived to Thee, I had never disobeyed Thee, never preferred anything to Thee! Would I may never more so offend Thee!" Say it from thy heart of hearts, and thou wilt know a joy, a joy, which if thou hast never so wholly given thyself to God before, thou hast never yet known, the joy of a personal love of God, as thine own God, the individual love of Jesus, Who saveth thee from thy sins. Blessed are they who so mourn, for they shall be comforted.

O God, who didst teach the hearts of Thy faithful people, by the sending to them the light of Thy Holy Spirit; Grant us by the same Spirit to have a right judgment in all things, and evermore to rejoice in His holy comfort; through the merits of Christ Jesus our Saviour, who liveth and reigneth with Thee, in the unity of the same Spirit, one God, world without end. Amen.

SERMON X.

The Spirit witnessing with our spirit.

BY

DANIEL MOORE, M.A.,

INCUMBENT OF CAMDEN CHURCH, CAMBERWELL, AND LECTURER
AT ST. MARGARET'S, LOTHBURY.

The Spirit witnessing with our spirit[a].

ROMANS viii. 16.

"THE SPIRIT ITSELF BEARETH WITNESS WITH OUR SPIRIT, THAT WE ARE THE CHILDREN OF GOD."

INTERPRET these words as we may, they must be allowed to announce a principle of unspeakable importance. The moment we hear them, we feel that we are dealing with a matter which concerns our life. The design of the passage may be to supply us with a rule for the trial of our own spirits,—to enable us to see whether we are in the faith or not; or it may be to set before our spiritual ambition one of the higher attainments of the saintly life,—the crown of an Abraham's faith, or the peace of an Enoch's walk: yet, on either of these views of the passage, a great blessing we

[a] The preacher thinks it necessary to say that this Sermon was prepared, not for the St. Mary's, but for the St. Giles's course, and consequently without the least idea of publication. On his arrival at Oxford, however, it was deemed expedient that he should occupy the place of the appointed preacher, who was unavoidably prevented from appearing at St. Mary's; and hence, at the Bishop's request, the publication of the Sermon.

feel it must be to be able to say, "The Spirit itself beareth witness with our spirit, that we are the children of God."

Let us glance for a moment at the connection of the passage. The Apostle had been speaking of the methods of adoption known among the ancients. In the case of a childless family, a stranger was adopted as a son; often a favourite slave, to whom the promise of freedom was given, and who was trained and educated for the position he was to occupy, and the family honours he was to enjoy. In like manner, those who are children of God by faith in Christ Jesus are described as being rescued from condemnation; emancipated from the bondage of sin and Satan; considered as sons and daughters of the Lord Almighty; and as such, placed under a course of spiritual discipline to qualify them for their future inheritance. Hence the servile and slave-like spirit is here supposed to give way, and the aspirations due to freedom and a nobler destiny are assumed to have place in the heart:—"For ye have not received the spirit of bondage again to fear; but ye have received the spirit of adoption, whereby we cry, Abba, Father." And then follow the words upon which I am asked to speak to you,—"The Spirit itself beareth witness with our spirit, that we are the children of God."

The topic falls in appropriately with that which it seems to have been the leading design of this course of sermons to set forth, namely, the paramount importance of the Holy Spirit's influence in the renewal and sanctification of the human mind. It is a doctrine of the Church, as a witness and keeper of Holy Writ, that the production of true religion in the heart is the result of an agency, absolutely Divine. And, in the passage before us, the same influence, requisite for the original production of the principle, is exhibited as equally needful for keeping in healthy activity all the exercises and emotions of an inward and spiritual life.

The two leading points to which the text requires that I should direct your attention are, first, the NATURE OF THE WITNESS which is here spoken of; and secondly, the FORMS in which we may expect it to be MANIFESTED.

I. In considering the nature of the witness, we must first advert to the spiritual relationship to be witnessed to, namely, that "we are the children of God."

This lies at the foundation of the Apostle's argument, that, by the power and grace of the Spirit, his converts had been emancipated from their former condition, and adopted into the family of heaven. As applied therefore to ourselves, it supposes a great fact, namely, that we are in a state of reconciliation with God; that we are the objects of Heaven's favourable regards; that there has been imparted to us, and still abides in us, that principle of heavenly life, which constitutes us "members of Christ, children of God, and inheritors of the kingdom of heaven." And this attestation is made, in the passage before us, to take the form of a grave judicial testimony. There is nothing to favour that mystical notion, which would resolve the witness of the Spirit into some preternatural intimation from above, some still small whisper to the ear of the inner man, testifying that we are the children of God; but the great fact is to be established on the joint authority of two witnesses, namely, the witness of the Holy Spirit and the concurring testimony of our own hearts.

And here we see, at the outset, the practical value of our fundamental doctrine, that the Holy Spirit is essentially and co-equally one with God. The believer's saving and confirmed reception into God's family is no overt act. It belongs to the deep, silent, unfathomed actings of the Eternal Mind; and we feel that He must be one, in and with that mind, who should be so far privy to its unuttered purposes, as to be able to assure us that we are numbered among God's elect. "What man knoweth the things of a man save the spirit of a man which is in him? Even so the things of God knoweth no man but the Spirit of God." This then is our confidence in the attestation. As being Himself a Divine Being, the witness is competent to speak. He knows the mind of God as intimately as we know our own. He searcheth all things. The deep things of God are open to Him,—the counsels of His will, the thoughts of His heart, the methods of His grace, the goings forth of His love, and peace, and reconciliation,—the Spirit not only knows all these, but is Himself the actuating energy of their accomplishment. And He "beareth witness that we are the children of God."

With this witness, however, the Apostle associates another, which, perhaps, we are to regard as not another so much as a medium for transmitting, to our own consciousness, the testimony of the first. This witness is the spirit of man himself,—the responsive testimony of our own hearts,—echoing the silent utterances of the Holy Ghost, and, in the experience of filial thoughts and tempers, assuring us of a re-instated friendship with God. Hence, in the way of direct and originating testimony, the human spirit can witness nothing. It is the interpreter of another: it is the passive recipient and reflector of a Divine impression: it is the witness *to* a witness; as if, according to the preferred rendering of some, the passage had stood, " The Spirit itself beareth witness 'to' our spirit, that we are the children of God."

What then do we mean when we say that a man has " the witness of the Spirit?" Well, generally we mean this,—that he has a happy sense of reconciliation to God, bestowed upon him by the Divine Spirit, but at the same time made manifest to his own consciousness by a perceived correspondence between the scriptural conditions of sonship and his own religious experience. No place is left for a credulous enthusiasm in this definition. The coincident verdict of conscience with the witness is assumed, and yet the witness itself is one which conscience alone is incompetent to supply. Conscience cannot testify that we are the children of God, except the Spirit reveal in us the existence of those moral dispositions, which prompt us to act as children act and to feel as children feel. Conscience makes the comparison, but the Spirit gives the power of perceiving the things compared: those things being the written Word, which defines what the characteristics of sonship are, and our own minds, which are to tell us whether these characteristics be found in ourselves. The perceived agreement between these two,—the Scripture calling and the heart answering, the Spirit of God in His Word insisting on certain commanded feelings, and our own spirits testifying that we have such feelings,—these constitute our double witness, our joint testimony in heaven and earth, our realized part in the experience, "The Spirit itself beareth witness with our spirit that we are the children of God."

To those who should object to this view that it virtually makes the witness of the Spirit to be nothing more than the witness of the Word, and that, consisting as it is thus made to do in a perceived correspondence between what the Bible says we *should* feel, and our own hearts testify we *do* feel, any man may obtain it for himself, we should answer first by a plain question, Could any inward witness to our salvation, any form of interior revelation, any whisper or breath from heaven satisfy us where the correspondence here spoken of was not found? Is it possible that the Spirit should contradict the Word, or testify to a reconciliation between God and the soul, whilst the Bible testified to some particulars in which God and that soul were not agreed? If not, the agreement set forth in our definition is a necessary element of the inward witness. The Spirit cannot speak two languages. His word must be the authorized exponent of His work, and His work must be evidenced by results, in accordance with the requirements of His Word. The Spirit is in the Word: and the witness of the Word is the witness of the Spirit.

Neither would it be fair to charge upon the view here given, that it reduces the witness of the Spirit into a mere deduction of the religious conscience. The deduction is in harmony with the witness, beyond question; but no man could draw it of himself without the aid of the Holy Spirit. This is the reason why many of the true children of God,—many, in whom the correspondence we are contending for, actually exists,—are not spiritually happy, but are desponding and cast down. They possess the required evidence of the filial state, in the agreement between the Bible description and the predominant bias of their desires and aims, but, through the depressing influence of despondency or doubt, it is as yet no evidence to them. Thus they have the hope of children, without the comfort of the hope. They could abide a trial of their spirits, as far as the verdict of a rational judgment, exercised on the statements of Scripture is concerned; but the actual assurance is not their own. And, until this cloud is dissolved, we cannot have the comfort of adoption. We may compare, and judge, and trust that there are found in us the marks of spiritual character, but we cannot, in all the deep, and full, and esoteric significance of the words, affirm that "the Spirit itself beareth witness with our spirit that we are the children of God."

II. We proceed, therefore, to our second enquiry, or THE FORMS in which this inward witness may be expected TO MANIFEST ITSELF.

i. And first, we may note that the testimony is *coincident* with, and not *opposed* to, our own consciousness. "The Spirit beareth witness WITH our spirit," says the Apostle,—not against it, not without it, not before it, but only in addition to it, and in corroboration of its testimony. All the acts and exercises of personal religion take place within. The graces of the Spirit, as they are called,—faith, repentance, hope, love,—are personal acts; the development of an active, intelligent spirit within, and their own witness that they descend from above. Apart from these evidences, therefore,—apart from the assiduous culture of holy principles and affections,—no witness of the spirit can be expected. Conscience has given an adverse verdict already, and its witness is conclusive. "If our heart condemn us, God is greater than our heart and knoweth all things; but if our heart condemn us not, then have we confidence towards God."

ii. We observe, next, that the witness of the Spirit is not *demonstrative*, but *evidential;* being, for the most part, gradually and progressively attained.

Here it may be competent to us to enquire, Is the witness of the Spirit to our being the children of God a privilege, always and universally enjoyed by men who have the spiritual mind, or is it a rule to be applied, deciding whether we have the spiritual mind at all? This is an enquiry, which plainly sends us back to the antecedent question, What is necessary to salvation? What is that attribute of moral character which causes that a sinner shall be pronounced justified in the sight of God? Because, if strong assurance be an element of this justifying quality, then the absence of this consolation would be fatal to our hope. Now the justifying quality, as we know, is faith,—by which we mean an act of trust, exerted objectively on the mediation of Christ, in all its parts, and on that alone. And justification actual is an instantaneous effect, ensuing closely on this act of exerted trust, as a fact; though it may be a long time afterwards before we are made conscious of our new condition, or can have had any experience of its resulting peace. We cannot make an uninterrupted assurance of our sonship to be an integral part of saving faith, without confounding two things, plainly distinguishable in themselves, as well as separable in the order in which they are experienced by the subject-mind. In themselves, we say the two things are distinguishable. The one is faith in something *done for* us, the other is faith in something *done in* us. The one is faith in the certainty of Christ's work itself, the other is faith in the certainty of our interest in that work. "The one" (to quote the words of Archbishop Usher) "is faith exerted on God's promises, the other is but a faith in our own faith." Nor can we consent to look upon these as light and unimportant distinctions. It is just the difference between a man's trust reposing on some fluctuating and uncertain feeling in his own mind, and its being made to turn absolutely on the fixed, finished, indefeasible efficacy of the atonement of our Lord. Let us not disturb the majestic simplicity of the Divine processes. Faith is the ordained instrument by which we are to lay hold on the promises of God in Christ; and it is to be exerted in them directly, because they have an objective certainty of their own. But if, instead of the promises, faith lays hold only on an inward witness, or secret persuasion, or any thing internal to ourselves, then, that on which it lays hold has no objective certainty whatever; but is certain only so far as the mind which apprehends it believes it to be certain. We cannot, therefore, without the utmost danger to our souls, allow the necessity of any mediate internal impressions to connect our faith with Him, who is its proper, sole, and all-sufficient object. Assurance, if made the ground of our confidence, will, in the day of trial, be found of all things the least sure. It must partake of the fluctuations of our physical and moral being. Whereas faith looks to an object which is without,—fixed, unchanging, and eternal,— "I know whom I have believed."

And it is a confounding of the order of spiritual

sequences too, this making assurance to be an element of a justifying faith. This order is thus laid down by St. Paul,—"being justified by faith we have peace with God." Faith, justification, peace,— this is the law of the divine procedure: the first, the conscious though divinely-prompted act of man; the second, the gracious bestowment of God; the third, a usual, but still, it may be, a long-delayed fruit of both. It is manifest that we may be safe, before we know that we are safe. We see a ship labouring, and ill piloted, on a dangerous coast. We see her make a point, at which the danger is over; but as the crew do not know this, their fears run on; and thus, while we are rejoicing in their safety, they live on in momentary expectation of that awful crash which splits the keel, and bears away the mast, and fixes the eye of despair on the in-rush of the wasting flood. And just so it will often be in our spiritual deliverances. We cannot realize the conviction that the point of danger is past. We dare not, all at once, discard our servile fears. Our ancient bonds cleave to us, and we fear to claim those rights of adoption, whereby, in all the spring and joyousness of an emancipated nature, we say, Abba, Father. Indeed, the Apostle himself is evidence that assurance comes not simultaneously with acceptable faith. For the time of the latter coincides with the moment when he resolved he would not be "disobedient to the heavenly vision;" so that, virtually, he was justified, or ever he came to the gates of Damascus. Yet, had he not, of many days, a sense of peace with God. And he wept, and prayed, and fasted, and trembled, and wondered, even while the shining hosts of heaven were hailing him, inaudibly, as "Brother Saul," and tasking the powers of their highest, holiest minstrelsy for that so great a sinner had repented.

Whilst, therefore, we put the assuring witness of the Spirit among promises which may be attained, and which, therefore, should be sought after, we are not to regard it as a constituent of our justification, or as an attainment invariably indispensable to the saving of the soul. It were to put a stumbling-block in the way of many weak brethren, to falsify the admissions of the most extended pastoral experience, yea, to unparadise the souls of many, whom all our charities oblige us to regard as now asleep in Jesus, to say that no man could be saved who had not at all times, perceptibly to himself, the witness of the Spirit bearing witness with his spirit that he belonged to the children of God. To be able to say this is a *privilege*, and a privilege which it will cause the loss of much comfort to ourselves, much honour to our religion, much praise to our God and Saviour, if we fail to realize: yet fail of such experience we may, under certain conditions of the religious life, and not fail of salvation. We may have the faith of reliance, when we cannot get the faith of assurance; and when, through the weakness of the flesh, we cannot lay hold on the witness that is within us, we may yet be saved by laying hold on the hope that is set before us.

iii. We observe, once more, that while the presence of the Spirit may be seen, as much in our most humiliating as in our most joyful experiences,—when we are in the valley as when we are on the mount,—such divine consolations are only to be looked for in connection with our own moral endeavours, and in the use of all divinely-appointed means.

All promises of spiritual influence are made over to us on these terms. Even with regard to the great promise, to Israel of old, of a new heart and a new spirit, we have it said, "I will yet for this be enquired of by the house of Israel to do it for them." Not without means, therefore,—diligent, earnest, persevering means, can we expect to realize this precious gift of "the witness of the Spirit." With regard to the means best suited to this end, if the view we have taken be right, that the mediate evidence of its existence to our own consciousness is a discovered resemblance between the revealed type of Christian character and our own moral experience, no practical direction can be more obvious than the duty of being much in the study of the two things to be compared—the word and the work, the book and the man, the saint's life and our life. Much shall we be aided in this work by a daily and believing contemplation of Gospel truth; an intent fixing of the mental eye on the revealed doctrine of Christ; a diligent gathering of materials for faith to believe, and hope to lay hold on, and love to cling to, and gratitude to adore. If we would have the witness of the Spirit, we must first learn the language in which His witnessings are given; and until the word of truth has been brought home to our convictions, the word of promise can give no peace to the heart. By searching the Scriptures daily, therefore, we are enabled to keep constantly before us the authentic and divinely-traced portrait of a child of God. And we observe its features, and mark its expressions, and see what a Christian is, and thinks, and feels, and does: till at last, imbued with the feeling and living spirit of the picture, we become like the thing we look on, and reflect the graces we admire.

And then, how further needful to this desired peace is it that we be much in *self-examination:*— seriously entered upon, impartially conducted, and diligently followed up by the repairing of all conscious deficiencies, and the renouncing of all discovered faults. Institute what forms of spiritual test we may, they must all be coincident with this, and all terminate in this,—an ascertained conformity of our desires, and aims, and principles of conduct with the revealed will of God. The Epistle of St. John abounds with Christian marks, yet as the Alpha and Omega of all proofs, he remits us to the one practical demonstration, "Hereby do we know that we know Him, if we keep His commandments." This will be to us a witness always. Is sin our hatred, holiness our delight, the favour of God our chief good? Can we bear meekly, forgive easily, help others cheerfully, and as cheerfully deny ourselves? Is there life in our devotions, sincerity in our obedience,—in our dealings with the world, do we maintain an unoffended conscience, and in our intercourse with God a simple and undissembling heart? Such testimonies, if given, will not long give forth their utterances alone. They will be confirmed by a voice from heaven. "The Spirit itself will bear witness with our spirit that we are the children of God."

But what if, as we have allowed to be possible, this confirming testimony in the way of consolation should not come? Why, then there is a reason for its not coming. God has further and more important ends in view for us than our spiritual peace. Here is one. "This is the will of God, even your sanctification." Keep your eye on that mark:—whatever furthers that, conduces to that, leads ultimately to the establishment and advancement of that,—must be better for you than all the inward witnessings and spiritual comforts in the world. At all events, if God see fit to withhold these testimonies, be assured it is for some reasons connected with your soul's growth and sanctification. What these reasons may be, I cannot tell. Perhaps He sees you would lean upon such comfortable experiences, if you had them;—would make a righteousness of them. Or perhaps the withholding is to keep you humble; to punish you for your past careless walking; to make you look more to the depth and sincerity of your repentance; to keep you from doing the work of the Lord negligently, and, as it were, thinking to have part in the joys of heaven before your time. Anyhow, we are sure the reason is a wise one, and a kind. The assuring witness of the Spirit is not a good thing for *you*,—at least not yet. God sees that you need the waters of sanctification more than the oil of gladness. More happy in your Christianity, you would be less watchful; more assured, less safe.

Wherefore, brethren, comfort one another with these words. I have said nothing to disparage the reality, the blessedness, the unspeakable privilege of this witness of the Spirit to our sonship. On the contrary, I cannot magnify its benefits too much. It inspires us with new love to God. It drops sweetness into the cup of our earthly enjoyment. It quickens all the powers of the soul to more devoted obedience. It strengthens the shield with which we beat back temptation. It bears up the heart against all outward suffering. It enables us to confront, without trembling, and without dismay, death, and the grave, and the opening door of the eternal world. And yet, I say, you may be destitute of this choice gift of God's grace, and still your soul may be safe,—safe in its hold on Christ, safe in its part in the covenant, safe in that unseen work of the Spirit, by which you are numbered with the children of God, and "if children then heirs, heirs of God and joint-heirs with Christ." Yes, brethren, look at those marks of the Holy Spirit's work which you find scattered over the face of this glorious chapter. They will be your best guides after all. The desires and tendencies of the heart towards God and goodness are the true tests, and if not belied by actual sin, they never did and never can deceive. They are the root. The assurance of sonship is the fruit. And the fruit will appear in its season. If you walk in the Spirit, and live in the Spirit, and are led by the Spirit, and look to be helped in your infirmities by the Spirit,—in due time you shall have the sealing testimony of the Spirit too,—" the Spirit itself bearing witness with your spirit that you are the children of God." Amen.

conditions of growth in grace
may means of grace as [preaching] not sown
use of due performance of duties
not neglect any duty [anc] of extra [bruisint] in others
that X [to which] blessing is attached
temptations overcome give strength
circumstances of our life [known to God] : useful [tous]
  pursuit of [holiness]
circumstances not sufficient — use of circumstances

SERMON XI.

Growth in Grace.

BY

W. C. MAGEE, D.D.,
PRECENTOR OF CLOGHER, AND RECTOR OF ENNISKILLEN.

Man a revelation of God
Difficulty of realizing man a God governed   (1) if Incarnation
Some denied made man's higher life unnatural   (2) — Inspiration
  — denied   ——— supernatural
  Bible testifies against both errors
            1 for supernatural
            2 agst unnatural
                (1) in pleadings addressed to our human nature
                (2) in exhortation "work out" "grow in grace"
                (3) grieve S. Spirit
                (4) us freedom of our will
                (5) [struck out] whole number of our doctrines

So pleading agst. despair & presumption
  both for brutes freed of growth of plant —
  we may stop plant growing & so soul also
What is perfection we should grow towards. Stature of
      in growth — grace — increasing likeness to X
  no other standard safe
L. of X must leave no room for presumption yet not for despair
  He shows us perfection not to mock, but that it may be
                                                        ours
Character of Divine life in us? — Sonship —
        Traced through life. This restores old promises
    renew spirit life by the degree in which the filial & loving spt
            of X is proving in us
Spiritual progress not always same course in all men

Growth in Grace.

2 PETER iii. 18.

"But grow in grace, and in the knowledge of our Lord and Saviour Jesus Christ."

THE Christian life, like the Christian faith from which it springs, is a great mystery. It is indeed but a part of that one great "mystery of godliness" which that faith reveals; for it, too, is a manifestation of "God in the flesh." Every renewed man is a real revelation of God. "God dwelleth" in him and "he in God;" and the Divine and indwelling Spirit reveals Himself in and by him to the world. "I in them and Thou in Me, that the world may believe that Thou hast sent Me," are the words in which our Lord sets forth the deep mystery of the Divine life in the soul of man. Not in figure or in metaphor, but in truest and most awful reality, are we made, by our living union with Christ, "partakers of a Divine nature." A nature which displays itself in words and works that are human, and yet that are also superhuman,—in a life which is that of a man, and yet which is life in God and with God.

Such a life is a great mystery. It presents, though in an infinitely lower degree, that difficulty which the idea of the Incarnation presents to our minds, the difficulty of conceiving of any real union of the human and the Divine; any union, that is, of God and Man, in which God shall still be truly and perfectly God, and Man truly and perfectly Man. However we may succeed in defining this idea in words, we find it all but impossible to realize it in thought. The moment we attempt to do so, it escapes from us, and we find ourselves excluding the thought of what is human that we may realize the idea of the Divine; or excluding the thought of the Divine, that we may realize the idea of what is human. We never can contemplate long that "strange sight," humanity indwelt by the Divine glory, without imagining that the inferior nature is consumed, or at least in some measure lost in the higher, the finite in the Infinite, the creature in the Creator, or without being tempted to doubt if the glory that we see be indeed the presence of the very God of heaven.

Such we know has been the history of the doctrine of the Incarnation. We know how, ever as men insisted on the truth of our Lord's divinity, they were almost insensibly led into denying, or forgetting, the truth of His humanity; or as they asserted the reality of His human nature, they were led into denial or forgetfulness of His Divine nature. And as with the idea of the Incarnate Word, so with the idea of the written Word: here, too, we have a union of the Divine and of the human, a Word that is God's word, and yet that is also the word of man. And we know only too well how some have insisted on the Divine authorship of this Word, until it ceased for them to have in any real sense a human authorship, until Prophet and Apostle were no longer men "moved by the Holy Ghost," but masks through which passed a voice not their own. And we know how others, revolting against this false conception of it, have insisted on the evident proofs of its human authorship, until they have come to deny that God is in any real and distinctive sense its Author too. And as with the idea of the incarnate Christ and the inspired Word, so with the idea of the Christian life. It, too, as we have seen, has its Divine and its human element, and it in like manner has been distorted by one-sided attempts to bring out either of these ideas to the exclusion of the other. We know how one school of writers dwell almost exclusively on the Divine and supernatural aspect of this life, until its natural and human aspect vanishes almost entirely from their descriptions of it; until it becomes an utterly unnatural and unreal state, in which man is seen the mere passive instrument of a creating and controlling Omnipotence.

By such teachers the science of the Divine life is and must be almost entirely neglected. They treat mainly of its first beginnings, or its more marked and striking crises when the Divine power is most startlingly manifested, and the soul may be seen stirred to its depths by the power of the Spirit. They would fain dwell always on the Mount of Transfiguration, or in the chamber of Pentecost, where the Divine Presence is seen in rays of glory, or in tongues of fire; but they seem to shun the lower paths of daily life, in which the Christian seems to walk only with the common light upon his path, and to speak the common speech of men. And the natural and necessary result of this exaggerated and one-sided statement of the great doctrines of grace has been, as violent and one-sided a reaction against them. Men have wearied of what seemed to them the unreality of such a religion; they have sickened of what they call its cant expressions, in which every word seems to lose its natural meaning and acquire some strange new one; they have insisted that man is something more than a machine; they have claimed for his reason and for his heart their place in the work of his own reformation; they have asserted for human life in this world its real worth and dignity. But they have gone beyond all this, and, asserting the human side of Christianity, they have denied the Divine. While proclaiming that the Christian life is not *un*natural, they have made it no longer *super*natural; they insist that there is nothing in religion really true or valuable but its moral precepts and its idea of God; they maintain there is nothing that is real in its duties that is not within the reach of all men; that the Heathen stands in this respect on a level with the Christian, and that we have but to obey the better instincts of our common nature, and we need no new birth, no higher nature, no divine grace.

Now against both these extreme views, each the exaggeration of a great truth, and each therefore a most dangerous error, the Word of God gives its clear and repeated testimony. In every word which tells us of our state of spiritual death, and of our absolute need of a resurrection and a new birth; in every word which describes that new birth as the work of the quickening Spirit who is "Lord and giver of life;" in every word which describes the newness of that spiritual life in its irreconcileable opposition to the old and fleshly nature which could therefore never have given it birth; in every word which ascribes the first motions of all that is holy in us—the inspiration of every good thought, the awakening of every holy desire, the suggestion of every holy purpose—to an Almighty Spirit dwelling in our spirit, and working in us both to will and do of His good pleasure; in every word which describes that new life as sustained by heavenly and mystic food, not fed "by bread alone, but by every word proceeding out of the mouth of God;" in every word which describes the Christian life as a progress from victory to victory over the world, and the flesh, and the devil, all unattainable* by the natural powers of the greatest man, all attainable by the weakest and lowliest possessor of this spiritual nature; in all these descriptions of this new life, from its birth to its glorious and completed manifestation, the Word of God sets forth for us an existence to which mere human nature, unaided and unchanged, could never reach, of which it could never even conceive; it testifies of this new creation, as of the old, that it "declares the glory of God and sheweth His handiwork."

But, on the other hand, equally clear, equally full, is the testimony of Scripture to the human and the natural aspect of this Christian life. In every word which appeals to our human reason, and pleads with our human affections, and addresses itself to our human sympathies; in every word which exhorts us to "work out our own salvation with fear and trembling," to "give all diligence to add to our faith" every needed grace; in every exhortation to heed and watchfulness against all spiritual enemies; in every call to the use of ordinances; in every institution and appointment of Christ's Church that makes us dependant for such ordinances on human ministrations; in every warning against neglect of these; and above all, in every warning against "resisting," "grieving," "quenching" that very Spirit of God which works in us with all the power of Omnipotence; in every such word which seems to make us in part authors of our own salvation, and altogether authors of our own destruction, which sets forth the awful power of the human will to shape the destiny of man for good or evil, does Scripture testify that the supernatural element of our new life does not overpower or destroy the natural, and that though God works *in* every renewed man, yet that every such man works also *with* God.

Such opposite statements are for the most part scattered throughout Scripture without any attempt to harmonize them, or to fit them into any one logical system. They are given us separately, that we may use them each in their turn as we need them; calling to our help in hours of despondency all words that tell us that it is the Most High God who is our Redeemer; calling to mind in our hours of carelessness and presumption all words that speak of our salvation, as a gift from Him that we may lose or cast away.

But there are passages in Scripture which bring together in one both these views of the Christian life, which express at once its supernatural and its natural, its human and its divine elements. Such a passage, for instance, as that in which we are bidden to "work out our own salvation," because "it is God that worketh in us to will and to do of His good pleasure." And such a twofold statement is given us in our text.

When the Apostle bids us "grow in grace," he tells us, on the one hand, that our life is from above; that to live it we need a grace—a free and gracious gift from God—a communication to us of "that thing which by nature we cannot have:" but then he bids us see that we "grow in this grace," that is, he tells us that this grace, though miraculous in its origin, is yet subject to natural laws in its progress. It has its growth, its normal and real development: a growth which we may help by our care, or hinder by our neglect, or destroy by our injurious treatment. The analogy here to the growth of the plant or the animal is perfect. The life of any living thing we cannot give. The vital principle that dwells in it is not of our creation. It has God alone for its author. But once that life is begun, once it manifests itself, as all life must, by growth, then we have power over it to shape, direct, and improve, or to distort and dwarf, or destroy. True it is that the creative power that gave it being at the first sustains it in all its after growth; that without this it would not grow: yet it is also true that the supplies of food or culture that are necessary to its growth are left to us to give or to withhold.

And this analogy, so frequent in Scripture, between the life of the soul and that of the plant, suggests an answer to the objection that is frequently brought by those who insist upon the irresistible character of Divine grace, that it is surely impossible for man to resist or defeat the purposes of God; that if His Holy Spirit have begun a work on our spirits, it cannot be that we should have power to prevent the completion of that work. Those who so speak forget that the same might be said of many another work of God. Every seed that He has created is made and designed especially to grow and to bring forth fruit after its kind. And yet we have the power to spoil this work, to frustrate apparently this design of God. The plant which He made to grow we can prevent from growing. The fruit which, according to His plan, it ought to have borne, we can say it shall never bear. And in both cases the answer to this seeming difficulty is the same. It is true that God works in the life of the seed as in that of the soul. It is also true that He has been pleased to set such bounds to the manner of His working that we may help or hinder the growth of either. It is not we who are in either case stronger than God. It is God who has in His original design left these limits within which our power may be exerted, and within which His will shall not overmaster ours.

But if the progress of our spiritual life depends so largely upon ourselves, if we are responsible for our growth or our decline in grace, then it is all important for us to have some standard by which we may measure this growth or this decline, some conception, that is, of what this life should be in its perfection. Every life tends to complete itself according to its own nature, tends to realize the true and perfect form of itself; and unless we know what that form should be, we cannot know how near it approaches or how far it falls short of this.

Where, then, is the perfect life by which we may measure our imperfections? Where is that form to which all our growth should assimilate us? You do not need, brethren, to be told where we are to find the example of a perfect life. We know that one such, and one alone, stands out among all the records of our race unstained by sin, undimmed by imperfection; the life of Him who "did no sin," and in whose mouth there was " no guile;"

the "beloved Son," in whom His Father was "well pleased." And we know that this life is the ideal and the type of our own. It is to this Image, faultless and glorious as it is, that we are "predestined to be conformed:" it is to the fulness of the height of the stature of Christ Jesus, high as it rises above all human excellence, that we are all yet to attain. To be like Him in all things, "grace for grace," to have His character fully formed in us, this is the perfection to which our Christian life ever tends, and which at last it is to reach. This perfection is not indeed fully revealed to us; "it doth not yet appear what we shall be;" that last development of our life, when grace shall pass into glory, is yet hidden from our sight. But we know that all the glory of it shall consist in its likeness to Him. "We shall be like Him, for we shall see Him as He is." Our growth in grace, then, is nothing else than our increasing likeness to Christ. To know if we are so growing, we have but to compare our life with His, to see how much of His Spirit dwells in us, how far "the mind that is in us" is the "mind of Christ;" to see how far we love what He loved, hate what He hated, desire what He desired; to see how far we can enter into that fellowship with Him which can only arise from increasing likeness to Him; how far we can understand and know Him, as kindred natures alone can understand and know each other; how far we have been baptized with His baptism, drank of His cup, shared in His death, and know the fellowship of

His sufferings and the power of His resurrection. It is only by such comparison of ourselves with Christ our great example that we can learn how far we are growing in grace. All other comparisons of ourselves with others, or with our past selves, are uncertain and dangerous. The standard of comparison in either case is so low that it is only too easy for us to flatter ourselves that because we have reached or even passed it, we have made great progress in the spiritual life. And so pride, and carelessness, and self-righteous complacency will check our growth in grace; or if we be given to despond, we shall be cast down often with as little reason, writing bitter things against ourselves, because we are not all we see others are, or all we think we once were; while, it may be, the very difference we see is a sign not of decay but of growth, not of decline but of progress. But no such danger arises from comparing ourselves with our true example, Christ. Infinitely above us as that example is; contrasting, in all its bright perfection, with our imperfect imitation of it; humbling us, as it does whenever we behold it, until we are ashamed even to think of our miserable shortcomings,—yet no despondency need mingle in our humility, for vast as is the height at which that life stands above us, we may, even as we scan it, have within us the assurance that we shall yet traverse it. Glorious as that ideal of excellence is, we may possess a pledge that we shall yet attain to it. For we know that He has not come to mock us with the display of a perfection that never can be ours. We know that that life of His, all-glorious as it is, He has lived, just for this, that it may be ours too. And we know, too, that as it has its perfection in Him, so it must have its beginnings in us, must have its gradual increase and growth, and that if we can recognise its beginnings, if we can only see in ourselves the first faint motions of the new and heavenly nature, then may we hope and believe that the life so begun, which is none other than His life, shall grow to that fulness of glory that we see in Him. Wrapped up in the acorn lies, from the first, all the strength of the oak. Hidden in the dark colourless root lies all the beauty of the flower. And the first small green leaf that peeps above the surface gives sure promise of all the future growth of flower and of tree. So, as we watch the first growth of the new life in us, as we recognise in it the essential character that marks it for what it is, even as we grieve to see that it is yet so small and weak, even as we tremble as we think of all the dangers that threaten its existence, and shrink from the thought of all the watchful care and toil we must bestow to foster and defend its growth, we may still in all humility and godly fear, yet with all faith and hope, rejoice as we hail the appearance of this work of God, and believe that He who has begun it will carry it on to the end.

And of the character of this Divine life in us—of that which, when we see it, distinguishes the new nature from all other—the Word of God leaves us in no doubt. That character is sonship. "To as many as believed on Him to them gave He power to become the sons of God." The essential principle of this new life, that which makes it altogether new, is that in it we regain our lost relation to the Father of our spirits, and become once more His children. "Behold," says the Apostle John, "what manner of love the Father hath bestowed on us, that we should be called the sons of God." "I will arise and go to my Father," is the first word of the new life in him who was dead and had been made alive; and in that word lay folded up the whole joy and glory of his return; just as in the word of selfish and unfilial separation, "Father, give me the portion of goods that falleth to me," lay all the sin and misery of his exile. "Abba, Father," is the first word that "the Spirit of adoption" whispers in our hearts. "Our Father," is the daily speech of that new nature which that Spirit bestows. "Father, into Thy hands I commend my spirit," is the last utterance of that nature as it enters into its last trial and undergoes its last change. It is this filial spirit which, all through its progress, rules and shapes the Christian life. It is the vital principle according to which growth in grace developes itself. It is this which, infusing itself into all the nature of the renewed man, changes it; not by bestowing new faculties or powers, but by restoring the old to their true use, and giving them their true aim and direction. It is this which ever wars against and expels the old evil lusts of the flesh. It is this which casts out disobedience from the will, and lawlessness from the desires, and impurity from the heart. It is this which, entering into all the religious emotions, makes them in like manner new: changes the "sorrow of the world" into "godly sorrow;" fear of wrath into fear of sin, and morality into holiness, and formal service into spiritual communion, and hope of heaven as an alternative to hell, into longing for the presence and the vision of God.

From first to last, then, this Spirit of adoption is the characteristic of the new life. "Beloved, now are we the sons of God:" here is the beginning of that life. "When He shall appear we shall be like Him:" here is its completion, and all that lies between these two is "growth in grace."

Now though, as I have said, if we measure our growth in grace by comparing any of our graces with the perfect example of those in Christ, we shall only learn how infinitely we fall short of them; yet if we measure it by the degree in which this Spirit of Christ, this filial and loving Spirit, is growing in us, we may find evidence of a real growth in grace. For we may find it not only, or perhaps chiefly, in any great increase of any Christian graces, or of all of them; we may find it rather in the grief that we feel because there is so little of such growth, in the earnest desires and longings for more grace, in the increasing consciousness of evil in us,—proofs not that the evil in us is increasing, but that our power of discovering it, and our pain at its presence, is increasing. Not always in the strength of our will, or the fervour of our love, or the freedom of our prayer, or the fulness of our peace, is the best proof given of our growth in grace. It may be given, though we fail at first to see it, in the discovery of the weakness of our will, and the coldness of our hearts, and the sinfulness of our lives. It may be, as we "mourn in our prayer and are vexed," and as we long in the very disquietude of our hearts to flee away and be at rest, that we have the best proof that things belonging to the Spirit live and grow in us, and that all carnal affections are dying in us. And, further, if it be this filial character of our new nature that really is its vital principle and rules its growth, we learn that we can lay down no fixed and rigid rule for the order of that growth. We may not say, for instance, that in every case the new life begins with contrition, and then passes through faith and assurance of forgiveness to perfect peace. No such rigid and uniform rule as this is laid down in Scripture. We might as well say beforehand in what order the leaves in spring should burst out upon the budding trees. In every true child of God all the phases of spiritual life will surely display themselves, but not all in the same order. In some the new life may begin in tears and agonies of sorrow, and pass on into smiles of joy and peace; in others it may begin in quiet and peaceful trust and happy service, to be disturbed, it may be ere long, with deep contrition of sin begotten, not of fear, but of love. It is the height of presumption to attempt to limit the manner of the Spirit's working, or to judge of His presence by any other test than the presence of the work of the Spirit, the conformity to the image of Christ. Wherever there is a Christ-like soul, there is Christ and the Spirit of Christ; wherever there is not this likeness, then, be the feeling or emotion ever so strong, or ever so strictly according to the prescribed rule, there Christ is not.

But if we are to grow in grace, we must know not only the tests but the conditions of such growth. Every life is fitted to exist only under certain conditions; it has its proper element, its proper food, and deprived of these it perishes. And as in the natural, so in the spiritual life, the supply of these is left in a great degree under our own control. The Communion of the Body and Blood of Christ, for instance, by which the soul is "strengthened and refreshed;" the "sincere milk of the Word," by which the newborn life in us should grow; the secret prayer, that opens for us an entrance into the treasury of heaven; the worship of the sanctuary, that brings into the midst of the assembled saints the presence of their Lord,—all these means of grace, through which fresh supplies of food from heaven should reach our souls, are ours to use or to refuse; we may, if we please, deprive ourselves of any or of all of these. We may in our slothfulness neglect them, or in our presumption despise them, and in each such case we know that our soul's health must suffer, our growth in grace must languish, if it do not altogether cease. Our first question, then, when we find any symptoms of decline in grace, should be, Am I diligently using all appointed means of grace, or have I neglected any one of them? Or, still worse, have I dared to choose between them, and to use some one especially to the disparagement of any other?—to put, for instance, private prayer in place of public worship, or hearing and reading the Word in place of the Holy Communion?—as if God had given us more means of grace than we needed; or as if we, not He, were to judge of what "food is convenient for us."

Or, again, we may be diligent in the use of all means of grace, and yet use them all amiss. We may so partake of the Lord's Supper as to eat and drink in it only our condemnation. We may so read or hear God's Word that it shall be to us a savour not of life, but of death. We may so pray that our prayer shall bring not blessings but judgment. We may so worship in the sanctuary that our service shall be an abomination, and our sacrifice an offence. And all the while we may be deceiving our own selves,—deeming this regular and formal observance of set duties in itself a proof of grace; dwelling, like the unloving elder brother, in the father's house, but dwelling there as servants, not as sons; serving God not for love, but for hire. In such a case there can be no growth in grace. All the rich abundance of the feast in our Father's House will profit us nothing, unless we sit down to it in the spirit of the repentant, forgiven, loving son, whose feast is not so much upon his father's gifts as on his father's love. If, then, while we cannot accuse ourselves of neglecting any one means of grace, we yet find in our souls no growth in grace, then let us see in what spirit, with what aim, we are using all these means. Are we using them as if the grace were in the means, and not in Him who gave them to us? Are we forgetting the Giver in the gifts, and seeking to have even these spiritual riches apart from God? If we are, and just so far as we are, will God withhold from us His best gift—Himself; and this very feast of good things He has spread for us be to our souls but as unsatisfying husks.

But we grow in grace not only by the right use of all means, but by the due performance of all duties. For the soul's health, as for that of the body, there is needed the vigorous and active use of all its powers. Disuse and decay are as clearly connected in the one as in the other. The grace which we do not exercise, like the limb we never use or the faculty we never exert, withers and dies at last. The duties that are appointed us are not arbitrarily chosen, they are each of them designed to exercise and strengthen some one or other spiritual faculty. And the neglect of any one of these can never be compensated by any additional activity in the performance of any other; we never can omit any one of these without injuring and weakening some corresponding grace, without making our Christian character one-sided and distorted, and therefore weak and sickly. And yet how strongly are we tempted to do this,—how constantly do we find ourselves making a selection among our duties, and excusing ourselves for our neglect of some, by extra zeal in the performance of others. For some, home duties are the plea for taking no part in the great works of the Church; for others, a noisy and busy activity in these is made the excuse for the neglected and deserted home. In their zeal for the Church or for their family, some have no time or thought for their own inner life; busy in watering the vineyards of others, they leave their own to lie waste and untended: while others, again, in their alleged anxiety for their own spiritual progress, profess to have no time or thought for aught beside: all of us only too ready to tythe mint and cummin in the doing of what we like best or find easiest to do, all of us only too ready to forget those other matters of the law,—those other duties which, just because we like them least, are for us the weightiest and most pressing.

And indeed as a rule we may take for granted, that the duty which we choose, by way of preference, is just the one that we least need to practise; and that the one we most neglect is just the one we most need to observe. We may be sure that it is because there is in the task we shrink from more of the cross for us, and therefore more of the discipline and training that we need, than in any other, that we are shrinking from it. And we may be sure of this too, that so long as we refuse to take up that cross, so long will He who has appointed it for us withhold the blessing which He has bound to it for us; so long will our spiritual life continue faint and languishing, even if at last it do not altogether perish.

But the endeavour "to fulfil all righteousness" helps our growth in grace for another reason. It leads us to the encounter with all unrighteousness: "The Spirit lusteth against the flesh, and the flesh against the Spirit; and these two are contrary one to the other." Against every duty stands its opposing temptation; against every grace its corresponding sin. Love strives with hate, and faith with doubt, and hope with fear, and gentleness with wrath, and obedience with lawlessness, and as they strive they grow. Stronger and still stronger does each grace within us wax, as it gains in its turn its victory over its opposite. And deeper and stronger too grows in us that essential element of our perfection—hatred of sin. We cannot be holy without this. The holiness of an unfallen being may consist in mere ignorance of evil; the holiness and safety of a fallen and regenerate being can only consist in the horror of evil that is gained by long and bitter experience of it. He who has known what it is to wrestle in agony with his bosom sin, or face with a desperate courage some terrible and haunting temptation; he who has known how the sin that he deemed slain will start up again mightier than ever, and the temptation once repelled with such desperate effort can return again and again;

he who has discovered how what seemed the very smallest sin as he indulged it, seems armed with a giant might when he attempts to oppose it; he who finds how the evil tenants of his heart, that seemed such harmless guests there, so long as they held undisturbed possession, can tear and rend that heart asunder ere they will depart from it; he who after some such deadly struggle has gained the victory at the cost of agony unspeakable, or has known the shame and the humiliation of defeat, he has learned, as none save he can learn, the "exceeding sinfulness of sin." And as he learns it,—as he sees all evil in him to be the deadly and loathed enemy of his life, which if he slay not, must slay him,—he has gained a growth in grace he never could have gained at lesser cost, for he has been taught to "love righteousness and hate iniquity," by the deep conviction wrought, by all his suffering, into his inmost soul, that righteousness is life and sin is misery and death.

But this thought, of the help temptation may give to our growth in grace, suggests the thought that there are conditions of that growth which seem to lie altogether beyond our control, helps and hindrances which are not of our choosing, but of God's appointing. All the external circumstances of our life, for instance; all those distinctions of rank, wealth, education, profession, social and family ties, that make such difference between man and man; these are, for the most part, not of our making, and these all we know largely influence our character and shape our history. How do these of themselves necessarily affect our growth in grace? How far is our spiritual life the "creature of circumstances?" We answer, 'Not at all.' Not in the very least degree does our growth in grace depend on anything without us. To say that it did, were to say that God could place us in circumstances which forbid our becoming holy, and yet required from us holiness; this were to make Him indeed an austere Master, "reaping where He had not sown, and gathering where He had not strawed."

Wherever the renewed man finds himself in this world, there is the best place for him, the place in which he is put, that in it he may grow in grace; "For all things work together for good to them that love God." "All things are ours, whether Paul, or Apollos, or Cephas, or the world, or life, or death, or things present, or things to come; all are ours, and we are Christ's, and Christ is God's." Here is the reason why nothing in our position need hinder our growth in grace,—for "we are Christ's;" and where we are He will be with us still; and so though we walk with Him through the furnace of temptation sevenfold heated, no smell of fire even need pass upon our garments: God is with us there, for "Christ is God's." Never let us, then, accuse our circumstances for our decline in grace; never let us yield to the vain and sinful wish to be elsewhere than just where we are; never let us forget that all that we dislike in our present condition, all that seems in it unfavourable to our growth in grace, is not only appointed of God, and appointed for this very purpose, that it should help our sanctification, but that it is also known to God; that He sees, far more clearly than we see, all the difficulties of our position, and has provided for us the "sufficient grace" to meet them. "I know thy works, *and where thou dwellest*," was His message to one whose dwelling was "where Satan's seat was." I know, that is to say, all in thy position that makes it hard for thee to serve Me; nevertheless that knowledge hinders not the warning, "Repent, and do the first works;" nor yet the promise, "To him that overcometh will I give to eat of the hidden manna."

And never let us forget either, that as circumstances and events in our lives cannot of themselves hinder, so neither can they of themselves promote our growth in grace. It is not the event, it is the use we make of the event,—it is not the circumstance, it is the manner in which we deal with the circumstance,—that makes us the better or the worse for it. Place two men in precisely the same circumstances, and yet how differently will they be affected by them. The danger that makes the brave man braver, makes the coward more timorous; the wealth that makes the spendthrift lavish, makes the miser more miserly; the loving devotion that wins in return the unspeakable love of one heart, only increases the tyrannical selfishness of another.

So is the effect of all God's providences upon our spiritual character; they are not self-acting, they are to us what we make them. "Trials come for our good," as we so often hear men say; but the good must be drawn by us out of the trial, or it profits us not. The same chastening that brings one sinner to "his God right humbly," drives another further from Him; just as the same fire that melts gold will harden clay. Even those outward conditions, then, that seem most beyond our control, are like those other means of grace of which we have spoken,—solemn responsibilities, trusts to be accounted for, talents to be improved, opportunities on which may hang eternal life or eternal death. A solemn thing, then, brethren, unspeakably solemn and awful, as well as a glorious and a blessed thing, is this Christian life of ours. For it is a life, the glory and blessedness of which consist in this, that through and in it all may be felt the presence of the indwelling, guiding, teaching, sanctifying Spirit of God. It is a life whose every event and circumstance may, by the power of that Spirit, be made to work for us an exceeding and eternal weight of glory, for it is a life which in its every event and circumstance might be made to minister to our growth in grace. But then how awful does this life appear, when we remember that in us lies the power of turning every one of its blessings into a curse,—when we think that according as we use them, may means of grace become means of destruction, and opportunities for good become occasions of evil, and merciful chastenings become hardening judgments, and all our history one long growth in sin, one long terrible ripening for the inheritance of sinners in eternal misery.

May God preserve us all from the sin of a wasted life! May God grant us all "by His holy inspiration to know what things we ought to do, and grace and power faithfully to fulfil the same!" Amen.

SERMON XII.

The Perfected Work of the Spirit.

BY

THE VERY REV. THE DEAN OF CANTERBURY.

The Perfected Work of the Spirit.

MARK iv. 29.

"When the fruit is brought forth, immediately he putteth in the sickle, because the harvest is come."

THE subject on which I am to address you, the perfected work of the Spirit, seems of necessity to include two separate considerations; the perfection of the Spirit's work here, and the perfection of the Spirit's work hereafter. And the wonderful words which I have read to you appear to take account of both. The fruit is one, the harvest is the other. *The fruit is brought forth*—that tells of the past, of the seed, and the springing up, and the blade, and the ear, and the full corn in the ear: *the harvest is come*—that looks on to the future, to the storing in the garner of God, to the fitness for the Master's use in all the glorious employments of the final and perfected state.

And it is to these two in order that I would endeavour to direct your attention; to the one indeed, which we see, at more length and with more certainty; to the other, which we see not, in fewer words, and more in the language of hope than of knowledge. First, let us speak of the perfection of the Spirit's work here on earth. Now it is very obvious and very easy to speak in language which may be perfectly true, so as to depreciate any even the furthest advance of this work of God's Spirit on the character of man on this side the grave. If we are to measure it by the pattern set us by Christ, if we are to compare it with the least conceivable degree of perfection in our glorified nature, it must appear scanty indeed. But I would not invite you thus to measure, or thus to compare. I would take the perfection of the Spirit's work on earth in reference to the actual material on which the Holy Ghost operates here below. I would take it as we find it, and try to ascertain what are its ripest and highest manifestations, and also when its work may be perfected, and we least suspect it. And surely this is the way in which we ought to consider the subject. The Holy Spirit has not come down on the Church for nothing. The estimate to be formed of His working is not to be a low and mean one. God is among us; God is working mightily in us; His arm is not shortened. That more excellent way, which came in when outward spiritual gifts ceased, has not proved a way of disappointment, nor a fool's journey. The perfected work of the Spirit has been carried on in a great multitude whom no man can number; is reached every day around us; nay we ourselves are, we humbly hope, advancing towards it.

What then is it? wherein does it consist?

The parable in the text may serve to guide us to an answer. It is found, when the fruit offers itself. It then has place, when the man is, according to his measure, filled with the blessed influence of the indwelling Spirit; when that degree has been reached in the way towards absolute perfection, further than which the Spirit, who knows what is in man, sees that he cannot advance: when that fruit of the life hangs ripe on the branch, to bring forth which was the work of that life.

Very various is this, both in kind and in degree; as various, as the ever-differing ages and places and dispositions of men. In some, the work is perfected at a time of life when in others it is but begun: in some, it is finished at a point of its progress which in others is but a halting-place for a moment. To us, it often seems to be cut short prematurely; but in reality it never is. It may be that to the eyes of man, a new race was beginning, a new line of duty scarcely entered upon, when the sudden accident, or the few days' illness, blighted the fair promise. But God seeth otherwise than we do. On some branches there was the fresh graft just inserted, and we thought of the wonder of the new leaves, and future produce not its own: but on others, the fruit hung ripe, and the great Husbandman knew better than we did that the time of harvest was come. The little child, blessed our home with its beauty, and its winning ways were gentleness itself, and it began to lisp its parents' names, and to run after the early flowers; and we wondered whether an angel was ever fairer, and blessed God for it night and morning, and were the better for its gentleness, and calculated on its companionship; and then God struck it, and it withered, and we wept over it a few days, and after that laid it in its grave. Yet even there was the Spirit's perfected work; that very beauty, that soul of gentleness, those winning ways, that dawning love for God's creatures, all these were the blessed fruits of that Holy Spirit who worketh in all according to the measure of all, that Spirit whose operations man is so apt to limit, and so inapt to comprehend. Yea, and from this upwards, all through the growth and the acquirements of the boy and the youth and the man, of the girl and the maiden and the matron, He who has begun the good work abandons it not in the midst, but ever brings it to its close, as He only sees when and how,—and gathers His wheat into His garner.

And as this perfection of the Spirit's work is not hindered by lack of time, so neither is it by disadvantage of station, or scantiness of earthly opportunities. For so may we have known the faithful domestic, found ever at his duty in the garden or the offices, with no thoughts beyond his daily work, and no learning further than to follow at family worship in his Bible, and he has become gray and bent, and on a day palsy has laid her hand upon him, and so he dropped out of his place, and his master comes and stands now by his bed-side, and ere long follows him to his grave. And another serves in his room, and to all seeming his trace is lost. Yet has that humble old man been a father in Christ, and in him too has the Spirit's work been perfected. And sayings uttered by him, when he walked in his narrow path of light, live in the memory of those who knew him, and shall come back to them in the day of sorrow, and light them through the dark valley; because they were of God, who dwelt in him by His Spirit which leadeth into truth, and gave him to utter things which the heart of man hath not conceived.

O in how many blessed examples like this is the Spirit's work perfected. And various are the ways which He chooses for carrying it on to perfection. By joy and by sorrow, by the toil of health and the patience of sickness, by meditations in solitude and the sweet trials of social life, in the dazzle of courts and in the humble monotony of retirement, by the presence and by the privation of the desires of a man's heart, in every occupation and when every occupation is gone, at all times and in all ways, is the holy work going on in the heart and character. Man knows it not; the heart itself cannot feel it, and cannot trace it minutely: but its fruits are seen;—more maturity of knowledge, more holy unction in speaking of the things of God, more conformity to His blessed will, increasing gentleness coupled with increasing wisdom. And as we have contemplated some lowly instances in which, notwithstanding appearance, the work was perfected, so may it be permitted us to contemplate others than which I know not whether there be any object more glorious, the sight of the exalted human spirit, furnished by acquirement of knowledge and trained by culture and discipline, dwelt in and hallowed by the Holy Spirit Himself. It is, thank God, a sight, though not of every day, still by no means uncommon. It is found not in seats of learning only, nor only among those who have read most and thought most, according to human methods. God has His own way of granting knowledge, and His own school for training those who are to be made wise unto salvation. It is granted to us sometimes to find, where we little expected it, this ripeness, and balance, and calm exercise, of the powers and affections, which results from long teaching by the Blessed Spirit; and sometimes also, where we most expected it. Sometimes it is in the invalid, for years laid by from active life, communing only with books and choice friends; from whom comes forth the sentence of wisest counsel as from an oracle of God; in whom the power of the Spirit is mighty, and the discriminating vision keen and unerring, and the deciding voice silver-clear and never to be questioned; in whom severity and love seem for ever to have run into one; from whom the kindest rebuke is the sharpest, and the sharpest the kindest. O what a bright sun in a household is such an one; what a preserving salt in a social neighbourhood. What a bulwark of strength for purity and for holiness do we feel it to be for our nation, when we know that there are very few households, and hardly any neighbourhood, without such an one to advise and encourage, and to rebuke; when we know that the outposts of the Church's army are studded with these bright sentinels ever at their guard, before whom the hosts of darkness crouch and tremble.

And sometimes again, we find this where we expected and looked for it; the pearl comes to our search, as it came without our search. We heard of giant powers of thought and ample learning sanctified by the salt of the sacrifice, and wielded under the guidance of the directing Spirit, and we half distrusted the report; for we knew how subtle and fatal are the snares of exalted talent, and how dangerous a temptation it is to dogmatize and to overbear, and how inaccessible commonly is one who knows to those who know not. But when we were brought near, our distrust turned into wonder, and our suspicion into hearty joy; for we found largeness and openness of heart, and wide entertainment of other men's views, and simplicity, and gentleness, and all-embracing love; we witnessed a mind which had risen, in the Spirit's upward leading, far above the banners of the hosts encamped in the valley;—which knew no party leader, and dealt with things for themselves, and as God seeth them. Nor is this, again, the only form in which the perfected work may be found where it was expected. It is perhaps the noblest example, but it must not exclude others. To rise above all partizanship, to keep the oneness of the Spirit in the connecting bond of peace, this is the furthest and highest attainment of the Christian character of love; but we may find the perfected work of the Spirit also where this is not. He who dwells in peace, and hears from a distance the sound of the conflict, and carries his mind and his affections above it, has a glory of his own, and a balanced perfection belonging to himself; but it is a glory also to mingle in the combat, and to contend for the faith; and in the champions of the various parties in Christ's Church we may sometimes also find this perfected work of the Spirit, — zeal united with love and guided by judgment, admirable temper, and forbearance, and forgivingness; jealousy for the honour of God and the maintenance of the truth; keen insight into the tactics and wiles of the opponents, and vast influence for good in a particular line and a circumscribed circle. Let us not doubt that the Holy Spirit is perfecting His blessed work in many such, who notwithstanding doubt and suspect one another. The history of the Church, and the history of our own experience, will bring before us abundant examples. In the very days of the Apostles themselves, no one can say that the spirit of St. James was identical in tendency with that of St. Paul, yet no one surely will say that the Holy Spirit's work was not perfected in both. And so, we may well venture to believe, has it ever been in the great controversies agitating God's Church; the Holy Spirit has worked in holy men severally as He would, imparting to one the spirit of fervent zeal, to another the power of skilful argument, to another the winning of the affections of men, but in all, according to the measure of each, filling up and perfecting His work.

This, then, is the sum of what we have said, that the Spirit's perfected work in this world is in each man in whom He dwells the bringing forth of his life's fruit, the advancing him to that for which God intended him, the wonderful guiding, and teaching, and building up, and tending, through paths other than man devised, by ways which his foresight never pointed out, of which it may be truly said in every one's case, what He doeth we know not now, but we shall know hereafter.

Let us not, however, pass on to that glorious consideration before we have noticed that as the Spirit perfects His work in every one of the sons of God, so is He doing also in that living temple which is the aggregate of them all, the Church, the Body in which He dwells. It is His work to prepare and deck the Church as a bride is prepared for the bridegroom. And as the other operations were mysterious, so is this. To us, and doubtless to every meditative Christian in almost every age, the Church has seemed rather to be in process of disarraying and disadorning; rent by divisions, with love waxed cold, become paralysed in her Master's work, loaded with fetters of worldliness and self-indulgence, she rather prompts the question, "Where is now their God?" than gives evidence of the perfecting of the work of the Spirit. Yet here again, God seeth not as man seeth. "The King's daughter is all glorious within;" and

He who hath begun His work in her will not cut it short, but will complete it to His everlasting glory. And then it will likewise be, as in the individual Christian life: when the fruit is put forth, when the Redeemer has seen of the travail of His soul and is satisfied, when the number of God's elect shall have been accomplished, then will He put in His sickle, because the harvest is come; and the perfected work of the Spirit here will be translated into the new and glorious state of which its highest measures have been but a poor and scanty foretaste.

And may we venture, before we conclude, to say anything of a matter of which we know so little as the Spirit's perfected work on that other side? Few indeed, and wholly inadequate, must be any words of man, to shadow forth things which it hath not entered into man's heart to conceive: still I believe we may with profit close our meditation with some surmises concerning it. And before all let us observe this,—that we cannot conceive of that continued work of the Spirit there, that it is otherwise, in one respect, than it is here. If we hold fast in any sufficient degree the continuity of personality in that final state, we must believe that as on this side death the Spirit filled each son of God according to his measure, so likewise will it be there. The measure of each will not be the same as here; but the relative difference may be the same. Immense, and to us inconceivable, will be the advance in each man's measure. Truly the first here are less than will be the last there. How will the glorious faculties of man's spirit expand as from bondage, when all sin is removed! How will all our energies nerve themselves afresh and spring up like a strong man that has burst his chains, when the new powers of the glorified body are given them to work with, and feebleness and sickness and decay have ceased to hem them in! How calm and unerring will be the judgment when we shall know even as we are known, and no shadow of bye purpose ever crosses our path, no bias of selfish consideration ever turns us aside! Yet this change will be, we may humbly believe, in each according to the place of each, in each according to the advance towards perfection here below. The babe here shall not become the pattern and leader there. It was Moses and Elias who appeared in glory; it is to the principalities and powers in the heavenly places that shall be known through the Church the myriad-coloured wisdom of God. There shall be those there who can stand and gaze nearer and more undazzled, and there shall be those who shall work God's will in the outskirts of the radiance from His throne: but in all shall the Spirit's work be perfected; in all shall this being of man, body, soul, and spirit, be advanced to its highest, and filled to the fullest with His divine indwelling and energizing.

And the Apostle has given us, in that great chapter which has been called the Psalm of Love, some glimpse of the conditions under which that perfected work shall be carried on. Knowledge shall be superseded by intuition, prophecy shall have ceased, —all partial, all progressive gifts shall be no more; but three conditions of thought and affection shall remain, and no exaltation nor glorification of man shall ever supersede them; and these three are faith, hope, love.

When the soul of man shall have been brought into the closest union with God,—when the purged human vision shall pierce through the veils which now hang before the Divine purposes, and far vistas of light lie open to its upward search,—still there shall ever be inner chambers unexplored, new avenues up to glory which shall look but as stars in the distance. None shall ever see how the converging threads of fate are folded around the divine Hand which holds and weaves them all. And therefore the perfected work of the Spirit there will ever be under the condition of *faith*—more unity with God's purpose, more reliance on God's wisdom, more resting in God's power, more persuasion of God's love.

And so likewise will it be under the condition of *hope*. I believe that one of the most blessed elements in perfect blessedness will be an unclouded future, in which hope may ever spread its wings of unblamed and unfailing adventure. The yearning of the soul, the progress ever onward, the to-morrow better than to-day,—are not these the very nerve and sustentation of our inward being? And in that perfect life they surely will not fail us. The good man's days here are no mean sample of what will be there. To-day was full of blessed deeds and thoughts; prayer and praise began it, prayer and praise ended it, and good works filled the space between; yet to-morrow shall be better, in that it shall see the carrying out of aspirations formed to-day. And so doubtless will it be there; and that perfected work of the Spirit, faultless yesterday, faultless to-day, faultless to-morrow, will never pall, will never want zest nor stimulus, because it will live and glow from day to day in the light of hope, with the rays of a future brightening and brightening for evermore.

And need I say, after what has already been said, that the condition of *love* is, above all and together with all, that of the perfected work of God's Spirit, as here, so there also?—there, where there shall be no jar of rivalry, no pang of jealousy, no bar of misunderstanding; where, among the infinite differences of the spirits and characters of the sons of God, the blending of the glorious whole shall be but more perfect for the distinctness of the individual parts. It is the world that loveth its own; it is of the world to love only those who are like ourselves and reproduce our own likings. It is of God to love that which we have not; to yearn towards the example of another portion of His likeness; to discern and recognise all that is good in all. And so will it be where that love abideth, which is the very uniting bond of all perfectness.

So will it be where the Spirit's work is finally and gloriously perfected.

O Lord God the Holy Ghost, perfect, we beseech Thee, in each of us here Thy present work; whether it be by the whispered accessions of Thy teaching in common daily life, or by Thy mighty voice sounding in the tempests of sorrow,—whether it be by a service prolonged to the last limit of man's time on earth, or against a call which we look not for in the midst of our days,—cause Thou us to put forth our fruit for God; that when the harvest is come, we may be gathered in where Thy work is perfected for evermore.

Now to the Creator Spirit, proceeding from the Father and the Son, co-equal and co-eternal in the ever-blessed Godhead, be all honour and glory, world without end. Amen.

BOOKS
PUBLISHED
BY JAMES PARKER AND CO.
OXFORD, AND 377, STRAND, LONDON.

Theological, &c.

THE BOOK OF COMMON PRAYER.
AN INTRODUCTION TO THE HISTORY OF THE SUCCESSIVE REVISIONS OF THE BOOK OF COMMON PRAYER. Crown 8vo., cloth, 12s.

THE FIRST PRAYER-BOOK OF EDWARD VI., compared with the Successive Revisions of the Book of Common Prayer; together with a Concordance and Index to the Rubrics in the several editions. Crown 8vo., cl., 12s.

BISHOP CLEVELAND COXE.
APOLLOS; or, THE WAY OF GOD. A Plea for the Religion of Scripture. By A. CLEVELAND COXE. Crown 8vo., cloth, 5s.

THE LATE BISHOP WILBERFORCE.
ADDRESSES TO THE CANDIDATES FOR ORDINATION on the Questions in the Ordination Service. *Fifth Thousand.* Crown 8vo., cloth, 6s.

WORDS OF COUNSEL ON SOME OF THE CHIEF DIFFICULTIES OF THE DAY, bequeathed to the Church in the Writings of SAMUEL WILBERFORCE, late Lord Bishop of Winchester. Collected and arranged by the late THOMAS VINCENT FOSBERY, M.A. Second Edition, Crown 8vo., cloth, 7s. 6d.

THE LATE REV. JOHN KEBLE, M.A.
OCCASIONAL PAPERS AND REVIEWS, on Sir Walter Scott, Poetry, and Sacred Poetry, Bishop Warburton, Rev. John Miller, Exeter Synod, Judicial Committee of Privy Council, Parochial Work, the Lord's Supper, Solomon, the Jewish Nation. By the late Rev. JOHN KEBLE, Author of "The Christian Year." Demy 8vo., cloth extra, 12s.

"They are prefaced by two letters of deep interest from Dr. NEWMAN and Dr. PUSEY. There is something extremely touching in the reunion, as it were, of the three old friends and fellow-labourers."—*Guardian.*

JEWISH INTERPRETATION.
THE FIFTY-THIRD CHAPTER OF ISAIAH ACCORDING TO THE JEWISH INTERPRETERS. I. Texts edited from Printed Books, and MSS., by AD. NEUBAUER. Price 18s. II. Translations by S. R. DRIVER and AD. NEUBAUER. With an Introduction to the Translations by the Rev. E. B. PUSEY, Regius Professor of Hebrew, Oxford. Post 8vo., cloth, 12s.

THE EPISTLES AND GOSPELS.
A COMMENTARY ON THE EPISTLES AND GOSPELS IN THE BOOK OF COMMON PRAYER. Extracted from Writings of the Fathers of the Holy Catholic Church, anterior to the Division of the East and West. With an Introductory Notice by the DEAN OF ST. PAUL'S. In Two Vols., Crown 8vo., cloth, 15s.

OLD CATHOLIC RITUAL.
A CATHOLIC RITUAL, published according to the Decrees of the First Two Synods of the Old Catholics of the German Empire. Done into English and Compared with the Offices of the Roman and Old German Rituals. By the Rev. F. E. WARREN, B.D., Fellow of St. John's College, Oxford. Crown 8vo., cloth, 3s. 6d.

"MERTON SUNDAYS,"
A Selection of the Sermons by the late Rev. H. W. SARGENT, M.A., of Merton College, and Incumbent of St. John Baptist: with an Introduction, &c., by the Rev. P. G. MEDD, M.A., Rector of North Cerney, formerly Curate of St. John Baptist, Oxford. Crown 8vo., cloth, 7s. 6d.

THE OLD TESTAMENT.
STORIES FROM THE OLD TESTAMENT. With Four Illustrations. Square Crown 8vo., cloth, 4s.

(477.1.10.)

THEOLOGICAL WORKS, &c. (continued).

REV. E. B. PUSEY, D.D.

DANIEL THE PROPHET. Nine Lectures delivered in the Divinity School of the University of Oxford. With a new Preface. By E. B. PUSEY, D.D., &c. *Seventh Thousand.* 8vo., cloth, 10s. 6d.

THE MINOR PROPHETS; with a Commentary Explanatory and Practical, and Introductions to the Several Books. By E. B. PUSEY, D.D., &c. In Six Parts. 4to., sewed. 5s. each Part.

Part I. contains HOSEA—JOEL, INTRODUCTION.
Part II. JOEL, INTRODUCTION—AMOS vi. 6.
Part III. AMOS vi. 6 to MICAH i. 12.
Part IV. MICAH i. 13 to NAHUM, end.
Part V. HABAKKUK, ZEPHANIAH, HAGGAI ii. 21.
Part VI. is just ready.

THE DOCTRINE OF THE REAL PRESENCE, as contained in the Fathers from the death of St. John the Evangelist to the 4th General Council. By the Rev. E. B. PUSEY, D.D. 8vo., cloth, 7s. 6d.

THE REAL PRESENCE, the Doctrine of the English Church, with a vindication of the reception by the wicked and of the Adoration of our Lord Jesus Christ truly present. By the Rev. E. B. PUSEY, D.D. 8vo., 7s. 6d.

The COUNCILS of the CHURCH, from the Council of Jerusalem to the close of the 2nd General Council of Constantinople, A.D. 381. By the Rev. E. B. PUSEY, D.D. 8vo., cloth, 7s. 6d.

ELEVEN ADDRESSES DURING A RETREAT OF THE COMPANIONS OF THE LOVE OF JESUS, engaged in Perpetual Intercession for the Conversion of Sinners. By the Rev. E. B. PUSEY, D.D. 8vo., cloth, 3s. 6d.

THE DOCTRINE OF BAPTISM, being No. 67 of the "Tracts for the Times." 8vo., cloth, 5s.

ON THE CLAUSE "AND THE SON," in regard to the EASTERN CHURCH and the BONN CONFERENCE: A LETTER to the Rev. H. P. LIDDON, D.D., Ireland Professor of Exegesis, Canon of St. Paul's. By the Rev. E. B. PUSEY, D.D., Regius Professor of Hebrew and Canon of Christ Church. 8vo., cloth, 5s.

F. GODET.

GODET'S BIBLICAL STUDIES ON THE OLD TESTAMENT. Edited by the Hon. and Rev. W. H. LYTTELTON. Fcap. 8vo., cloth, 6s.

VERY REV. JOHN W. BURGON, B.D., Dean of Chichester.

THE LAST TWELVE VERSES OF THE GOSPEL ACCORDING TO S. MARK Vindicated against Recent Critical Objectors and Established, by JOHN W. BURGON, B.D., Dean of Chichester. With Facsimiles of Codex ℵ and Codex L. 8vo., cloth, 12s.

LATE REV. ARTHUR WEST HADDAN, B.D.

THE REMAINS of the late ARTHUR WEST HADDAN, B.D., Rector of Barton-on-the-Heath. Edited by the late Right Rev. A. P. FORBES, D.C.L., Bishop of Brechin. 8vo., cloth, price 12s.

REV. G. WILDON PIERITZ.

THE GOSPELS FROM A RABBINICAL POINT OF VIEW, shewing the Harmony of the Four Evangelists on the subject of our Lord's Last Supper, and the Bearing of the Laws and Customs of the Jews on the Language of the Gospels. By the Rev. G. WILDON PIERITZ, M.A. Cr. 8vo., limp cloth, 3s.

REV. CANON TREVOR, D.D., M.A.

THE CATHOLIC DOCTRINE OF THE SACRIFICE AND PARTICIPATION OF THE HOLY EUCHARIST. By GEORGE TREVOR, D.D., M.A., Canon of York; Rector of Beeford. Second Edition, revised and enlarged. Crown 8vo., cloth, 10s. 6d.

THE LATE REV. J. KEBLE, M.A.

LETTERS OF SPIRITUAL COUNSEL AND GUIDANCE. By the late Rev. J. KEBLE, M.A., Vicar of Hursley. Edited, with a New Preface, by R. F. WILSON, M.A., Vicar of Rownhams, &c. Third Edition, much enlarged, Post 8vo., cloth, 6s.

ON EUCHARISTICAL ADORATION. By the late Rev. JOHN KEBLE, M.A., Vicar of Hursley.—With Considerations suggested by a Pastoral Letter on the Doctrine of the Most Holy Eucharist. Cheap Edition, 24mo., sewed, 2s.

THE LATE BISHOP OF BRECHIN.

AN EXPLANATION OF THE THIRTY-NINE ARTICLES. With an Epistle Dedicatory to the Rev. E. B. PUSEY, D.D. By A. P. FORBES, D.C.L., Bishop of Brechin. Second Edition, Crown 8vo., cloth, 12s.

A SHORT EXPLANATION OF THE NICENE CREED, for the Use of Persons beginning the Study of Theology. By ALEXANDER PENROSE FORBES, D.C.L., Bishop of Brechin. Second Edition. Crown 8vo., cloth, 6s.

THE LORD BISHOP OF SALISBURY.

THE ADMINISTRATION OF THE HOLY SPIRIT IN THE BODY OF CHRIST. The Bampton Lectures for 1868. By GEORGE MOBERLY, D.C.L., Lord Bishop of Salisbury. 2nd Edit. Crown 8vo., cloth, 7s. 6d.

SERMONS ON THE BEATITUDES, with others mostly preached before the University of Oxford. By GEORGE MOBERLY, D.C.L. Third Edition. Crown 8vo., cloth, 7s. 6d.

REV. WILLIAM BRIGHT, D.D.

A HISTORY OF THE CHURCH, from the Edict of Milan, A.D. 313, to the Council of Chalcedon, A.D. 451. Second Edition. Post 8vo., 10s. 6d.

JOHN DAVISON, B.D.

DISCOURSES ON PROPHECY. In which are considered its Structure, Use, and Inspiration. By JOHN DAVISON, B.D. A New Edition. 8vo., cloth, 9s.

THE LATE ARCHDEACON FREEMAN.

THE PRINCIPLES OF DIVINE SERVICE; or, An Inquiry concerning the True Manner of Understanding and Using the Order for Morning and Evening Prayer, and for the Administration of the Holy Communion in the English Church. A New Edition. 2 vols., 8vo., cloth, 16s.

CATENA AUREA.

CATENA AUREA. A Commentary on the Four Gospels, collected out of the Works of the Fathers by S. THOMAS AQUINAS. Uniform with the Library of the Fathers. Re-issue. Complete in 6 vols. 8vo., cloth, £2 2s.

REV. DR. IRONS.

CHRISTIANITY AS TAUGHT BY S. PAUL. The Bampton Lectures for 1870. To which is added an Appendix of the Continuous Sense of S. Paul's Epistles; with Notes and Metalegomena. Second Edition, with New Preface, 8vo., with Map, cloth, 9s.

REV. I. GREGORY SMITH, M.A.

CHARACTERISTICS OF CHRISTIAN MORALITY. The Bampton Lectures for 1873. Second Edition, Crown 8vo., cloth, 3s. 6d.

BEDE'S ECCLESIASTICAL HISTORY.

BEDE'S ECCLESIASTICAL HISTORY OF THE ENGLISH NATION. A New Translation by the Rev. L. GIDLEY, M.A., Chaplain of St. Nicholas', Salisbury. Crown 8vo., cloth, 6s.

REV. D. WATERLAND, D.D.

A CRITICAL HISTORY OF THE ATHANASIAN CREED, by the Rev. DANIEL WATERLAND, D.D. Edited by the Rev. J. R. KING, M.A. Fcap. 8vo., cloth, 5s.

THE CONSTITUTIONS AND CANONS ECCLESIASTICAL OF THE CHURCH OF ENGLAND, Referred to their Original Sources, and Illustrated with Explanatory Notes. By MACKENZIE E. C. WALCOTT, B.D., F.S.A., Præcentor and Prebendary of Chichester. Fcap. 8vo., cloth, 4s.

THE PASTORAL RULE OF ST. GREGORY. Sancti Gregorii Papæ Regulæ Pastoralis Liber, ad Johannem Episcopum Civitatis Ravennæ. With an English Translation. By the Rev. H. R. BRAMLEY, M.A., Fellow of Magdalen College, Oxford. Fcap. 8vo., cloth, 6s.

THE DEFINITIONS OF THE CATHOLIC FAITH and Canons of Discipline of the first four General Councils of the Universal Church. In Greek and English. Fcap. 8vo., cloth, 2s. 6d.

DE FIDE ET SYMBOLO: Documenta quædam nec non Aliquorum SS. Patrum Tractatus. Edidit CAROLUS A. HEURTLEY, S.T.P., Dom. Margaretæ Prælector, et Ædis Christi Canonicus. Fcap. 8vo., cloth, 4s. 6d.

S. AURELIUS AUGUSTINUS, Episcopus Hipponensis, de Catechizandis Rudibus, de Fide Rerum quæ non videntur, de Utilitate Credendi. In Usum Juniorum. Edidit C. MARRIOTT, S.T.B., Olim Coll. Oriel. Socius. *New Edition.* Fcap. 8vo., cloth, 3s. 6d.

ANALECTA CHRISTIANA, In usum Tironum. Excerpta, Epistolæ, &c., ex EUSEBII, &c.; S. IGNATII Epistolæ ad Smyrnæos et ad Polycarpum; E. S. CLEMENTIS ALEXANDRI Pædagogo excerpta; S. ATHANASII Sermo contra Gentes. Edidit et Annotationibus illustravit C. MARRIOTT, S.T.B. 8vo., 10s. 6d.

CUR DEUS HOMO, or Why God was made Man; by ST. ANSELM. Translated into English, with an Introduction, &c. *Second Edition.* Fcap. 8vo., 2s. 6d.

THE BOOK OF RATRAMN the Priest and Monk of Corbey, commonly called Bertram, on the Body and Blood of the Lord. (Latin and English.) To which is added AN APPENDIX, containing the Saxon Homily of Ælfric. Fcap. 8vo. *[Nearly ready.*

OXFORD SERIES OF DEVOTIONAL WORKS. Fcap. 8vo.

The Imitation of Christ.
FOUR BOOKS. By THOMAS A KEMPIS. Cloth, 4s.

Andrewes' Devotions.
DEVOTIONS. By the Right Rev. Father in God, LAUNCELOT ANDREWES. Translated from the Greek and Latin, and arranged anew. Antique cloth, 5s.

Taylor's Holy Living.
THE RULE AND EXERCISES OF HOLY LIVING. By BISHOP JEREMY TAYLOR. Antique cloth, 4s.

Taylor's Holy Dying.
THE RULE AND EXERCISES OF HOLY DYING. By BISHOP JEREMY TAYLOR. Antique cloth, 4s.

Taylor's Golden Grove.
THE GOLDEN GROVE; a Choice Manual, containing what is to be Believed, Practised, and Desired, or Prayed for. By BISHOP JEREMY TAYLOR. Printed uniform with "Holy Living and Holy Dying." Antique cloth, 3s. 6d.

Sutton's Meditations.
GODLY MEDITATIONS UPON THE MOST HOLY SACRAMENT OF THE LORD'S SUPPER. By CHRISTOPHER SUTTON, D.D., late Prebend of Westminster. A new Edition. Antique cloth, 5s.

Wilson's Sacra Privata.
THE PRIVATE MEDITATIONS, DEVOTIONS, and PRAYERS of the Right Rev. T. WILSON, D.D., Lord Bishop of Sodor and Man. Now first printed entire. Cloth, 4s.

Laud's Devotions.
THE PRIVATE DEVOTIONS of DR. WILLIAM LAUD, Archbishop of Canterbury, and Martyr. Antique cloth, 5s.

Spinckes' Devotions.
TRUE CHURCH OF ENGLAND MAN'S COMPANION IN THE CLOSET; or, a complete Manual of Private Devotions, collected from the Writings of eminent Divines of the Church of England. Floriated borders, antique cloth, 4s.

Ancient Collects.
ANCIENT COLLECTS AND OTHER PRAYERS. Selected for Devotional use from various Rituals. By WM. BRIGHT, D.D. Antique cloth, 5s.

Devout Communicant.
THE DEVOUT COMMUNICANT, exemplified in his Behaviour before, at, and after the Sacrament of the Lord's Supper: Practically suited to all the Parts of that Solemn Ordinance. 7th Edition, revised. Fcap. 8vo., toned paper, red lines, cloth, 4s.

ΕΙΚΩΝ ΒΑΣΙΛΙΚΗ.
THE PORTRAITURE OF HIS SACRED MAJESTY KING CHARLES I. in his Solitudes and Sufferings. Ant. cloth, 5s.

DEVOTIONAL.

THE SERVICE-BOOK OF THE CHURCH OF ENGLAND, arranged according to the New Table of Lessons. Crown 8vo., roan, 12s.; calf antique or calf limp, 16s.; limp morocco or best morocco, 18s.

ANNUS DOMINI. A Prayer for each Day of the Year, founded on a Text of Holy Scripture. By CHRISTINA G. ROSSETTI. 32mo., cloth, 3s. 6d.

DEVOTIONS BEFORE AND AFTER HOLY COMMUNION. With Prefatory Note by KEBLE. Sixth Edition, in red and black, on toned paper, 32mo., cloth, 2s.

The above, with the Service, 32mo., cloth, 2s. 6d.

INSTRUCTIONS ON THE HOLY EUCHARIST, AND DEVOTIONS FOR HOLY COMMUNION, being Part V. of the Clewer Manuals, by Rev. T. T. CARTER, M.A., Rector of Clewer. 18mo., cloth, 2s.

PARABLES AND MEDITATIONS FOR SUNDAYS AND HOLY DAYS. Translated from the German by A. GURNEY. Post 8vo., toned paper, cloth, 3s. 6d.

THE EVERY-DAY COMPANION. By the Rev. W. H. RIDLEY, M.A., Rector of Hambleden, Bucks. Fcap. 8vo., cloth, 3s.

THE LIFE OF JESUS CHRIST IN GLORY: Daily Meditations, from Easter Day to the Wednesday after Trinity Sunday. By NOUET. Translated from the French, and adapted to the Use of the English Church. *Third Thousand.* 12mo., cloth, 6s.

A GUIDE FOR PASSING ADVENT HOLILY. By AVRILLON. Translated from the French, and adapted to the use of the English Church. *New Edition.* Fcap. 8vo., cloth, 5s.

A GUIDE FOR PASSING LENT HOLILY. By AVRILLON. Translated from the French, and adapted to the use of the English Church. Fourth Edition. Fcap. 8vo., cloth, 6s.

MEDITATIONS FOR THE FORTY DAYS OF LENT. With a Prefatory Notice by the ARCHBISHOP OF DUBLIN. 18mo., cloth, 2s. 6d.

OF THE IMITATION OF CHRIST. FOUR BOOKS. By THOMAS A KEMPIS. A New Edition revised. On toned paper, with red border-lines, &c. Small 4to., cloth, 12s. Also, printed in red and black. Fcap., cloth, 4s.

DE IMITATIONE CHRISTI. Libri Quatuor. Fcap. 8vo., cloth, 5s.; 16mo., cloth, 2s.

THE INNER LIFE. Hymns on the "Imitation of Christ," by THOMAS A'KEMPIS; designed especially for Use at Holy Communion. By the Author of "Thoughts from a Girl's Life," &c. Fcap. 8vo., cloth, 3s.

DAILY STEPS TOWARDS HEAVEN; or, Practical Thoughts on the Gospel History, for every day in the year. With Titles and Characters of Christ. 32mo., roan, 2s. 6d. Large type edition, Crown 8vo., cloth, 5s.

EVENING WORDS. Brief Meditations on the Introductory Portion of our Lord's Last Discourse with His Disciples. 16mo., cloth, 2s.

THOUGHTS DURING SICKNESS. By ROBERT BRETT, Author of "The Doctrine of the Cross," &c. Fcap. 8vo., limp cloth, 1s. 6d.

THE PASTOR IN HIS CLOSET; or, A Help to the Devotions of the Clergy. By JOHN ARMSTRONG, D.D., late Lord Bishop of Grahamstown. *Third Edition.* Fcap. 8vo., cloth, 2s.

BREVIATES FROM HOLY SCRIPTURE, arranged for use by the Bed of Sickness. By the Rev. G. ARDEN, M.A., Rector of Winterborne-Came; Domestic Chaplain to the Right Hon. the Earl of Devon. *2nd Ed.* Fcap. 8vo., 2s.

SHORT READINGS FOR SUNDAY. By the Author of "Footprints in the Wilderness." With Twelve Illustrations on Wood. Third Thousand, Square Crown 8vo., cloth, 3s. 6d.

DEVOTIONS FOR A TIME OF RETIREMENT AND PRAYER FOR THE CLERGY. New Edition, revised. Fcap. 8vo., cloth, 1s.

SERMONS, &c.

PAROCHIAL SERMONS. By E. B. Pusey, D.D. Vol. I. From Advent to Whitsuntide. *Seventh Edition.* 8vo., cloth, 6s. Vol. II., 8vo., cl., 6s. ———— Vol. III. Reprinted from "Plain Sermons by Contributors to Tracts for the Times." Revised Edition. 8vo., cloth, 6s.

PAROCHIAL SERMONS preached and printed on Various Occasions, 1832—1850. By E. B. PUSEY, D.D. 8vo., cloth, 6s.

SERMONS preached before the UNIVERSITY OF OXFORD between A.D. 1859 and 1872. By E. B. PUSEY, D.D. 8vo., cloth, 6s.

LENTEN SERMONS preached chiefly to Young Men at the Universities, between A.D. 1868 and 1874. By E. B. PUSEY, D.D. 8vo., cloth, 6s.

ILLUSTRATIONS OF FAITH. Eight Plain Sermons, by the late Rev. EDWARD MONRO. Fcap. 8vo., cloth, 2s. 6d.

Uniform, and by the same Author,

PLAIN SERMONS ON THE BOOK OF COMMON PRAYER. Fcap. 8vo., cloth, 5s.

SERMONS ON NEW TESTAMENT CHARACTERS. Fcap. 8vo., cloth, 4s.

HISTORICAL AND PRACTICAL SERMONS ON THE SUFFERINGS AND RESURRECTION OF OUR LORD. 2 vols., Fcap. 8vo., cloth, 10s.

CHRISTIAN SEASONS.—Short and Plain Sermons for every Sunday and Holyday throughout the Year. Edited by the late Bishop of Grahamstown. 4 vols., Fcap. 8vo., cloth, 10s. Second Series, 4 vols., Fcap. 8vo., cloth, 10s.

SHORT SERMONS FOR FAMILY READING, following the Order of the Christian Seasons. By the Rev. J. W. BURGON, B.D., Dean of Chichester. 2 vols., Fcap. 8vo., cl., 8s. 2nd Series, 2 vols., Fcap. 8vo., cl., 8s.

PAROCHIAL SERMONS. By the late JOHN ARMSTRONG, D.D., Lord Bishop of Grahamstown. Fcap. 8vo., cl., 5s.

SERMONS FOR FASTS AND FESTIVALS. By the late JOHN ARMSTRONG, D.D. A new Edition. Fcap. 8vo., 5s.

SERMONS FOR THE CHRISTIAN YEAR. By the Rev. JOHN KEBLE, Author of "The Christian Year."

ADVENT TO CHRISTMAS. 8vo., cl., 6s.

ASH-WEDNESDAY TO HOLY WEEK. 8vo., cloth, 6s.

CHRISTMAS AND EPIPHANY. 8vo., cloth, 6s.

HOLY WEEK. 8vo., cloth, 6s.

EASTER TO ASCENSION DAY. 8vo., cloth, 6s.

ASCENSION DAY TO TRINITY SUNDAY inclusive. 8vo., cloth, 6s.

There remain, to follow at intervals,

SEPTUAGESIMA TO LENT. | SERMONS FOR THE TRINITY SEASON.

SERMONS FOR SAINTS' DAYS.

VILLAGE SERMONS ON THE BAPTISMAL SERVICE. By the Rev. JOHN KEBLE, M.A., Author of "The Christian Year." 8vo., cloth, 5s.

SERMONS OCCASIONAL AND PAROCHIAL. By the Rev. JOHN KEBLE, M.A. 8vo., cloth, 12s.

XX. SHORT ALLEGORICAL SERMONS. By the Rev. BEAUCHAMP K. W. PEARSE, M.A., Rector of Ascot, Staines, and Rev. WALTER AUGUSTUS GRAY, M.A., Vicar of Arksey, Yorkshire. *Fourth Edition,* Fcap., cloth, 2s. 6d. *Fifth Edition,* Fcap. 8vo., sewed, 1s.

SERMONS AND ESSAYS ON THE APOSTOLICAL AGE. By the Very Rev. ARTHUR PENRHYN STANLEY, D.D., Dean of Westminster, and Corresponding Member of the Institute of France. *Third Edition, revised.* Crown 8vo., cloth, 7s. 6d.

CHRIST'S SOLDIERS. Sermons preached at St. George's Garrison Church, Woolwich, by the Rev. W. F. SHORT, M.A., Fellow of New College, Oxford; Chaplain to the Royal Military Academy, Woolwich. Cr. 8vo., cl., 5s.

WORDS AT COMMUNION-TIME. Short Sermons preached at Celebrations of Holy Communion. By WALTER FRANCIS ELGIE, M.A., Curate in Charge of Otterbourne, Hants. Fcap. 8vo., cloth, 3s. 6d.

OXFORD LENT SERMONS, 1859, 65, 6, 7, 8, 9, 70. 8vo., cloth, 5s. each.

Works of the Standard English Divines,

PUBLISHED IN THE LIBRARY OF ANGLO-CATHOLIC THEOLOGY,

AT THE FOLLOWING PRICES IN CLOTH.

ANDREWES' (BP.) COMPLETE WORKS. 11 vols., 8vo., £3 7s.
    THE SERMONS. (Separate.) 5 vols., £1 15s.

BEVERIDGE'S (BP.) COMPLETE WORKS. 12 vols., 8vo., £4 4s.
    THE ENGLISH THEOLOGICAL WORKS. 10 vols., £3 10s.

BRAMHALL'S (ABP.) WORKS, WITH LIFE AND LETTERS, &c. 5 vols., 8vo., £1 15s. (Vol. 2 cannot be sold separately.)

BULL'S (BP.) HARMONY ON JUSTIFICATION. 2 vols., 8vo., 10s.
——————— DEFENCE OF THE NICENE CREED. 2 vols., 10s.
——————— JUDGMENT OF THE CATHOLIC CHURCH. 5s.

COSIN'S (BP.) WORKS COMPLETE. 5 vols., 8vo., £1 10s.

CRAKANTHORP'S DEFENSIO ECCLESIÆ ANGLICANÆ. 8vo., 7s.

FRANK'S SERMONS. 2 vols., 8vo., 10s.

FORBES' CONSIDERATIONES MODESTÆ. 2 vols., 8vo., 12s.

GUNNING'S PASCHAL, OR LENT FAST. 8vo, 6s.

HAMMOND'S PRACTICAL CATECHISM. 8vo., 5s.
——————— MISCELLANEOUS THEOLOGICAL WORKS. 5s.
——————— THIRTY-ONE SERMONS. 2 Parts. 10s.

HICKES'S TWO TREATISES ON THE CHRISTIAN PRIESTHOOD. 3 vols., 8vo., 15s.

JOHNSON'S (JOHN) THEOLOGICAL WORKS. 2 vols., 8vo., 10s.
——————— ENGLISH CANONS. 2 vols., 12s.

LAUD'S (ABP.) COMPLETE WORKS. 7 vols., (9 Parts,) 8vo., £2 17s.

L'ESTRANGE'S ALLIANCE OF DIVINE OFFICES. 8vo., 6s.

MARSHALL'S PENITENTIAL DISCIPLINE. (This volume cannot be sold separate from the complete set.)

NICHOLSON'S (BP.) EXPOSITION OF THE CATECHISM. (This volume cannot be sold separate from the complete set.)

OVERALL'S (BP.) CONVOCATION-BOOK OF 1606. 8vo., 5s.

PEARSON'S (BP.) VINDICIÆ EPISTOLARUM S. IGNATII. 2 vols. 8vo., 10s.

THORNDIKE'S (HERBERT) THEOLOGICAL WORKS COMPLETE. 6 vols., (10 Parts,) 8vo., £2 10s.

WILSON'S (BP.) WORKS COMPLETE. With LIFE, by Rev. J. KEBLE. 7 vols., (8 Parts,) 8vo., £3 3s.

A complete set, £21.

POETRY, &c.

THE AUTHORIZED EDITIONS OF
THE CHRISTIAN YEAR,

With the Author's latest Corrections and Additions.

NOTICE.—Messrs. PARKER are the sole Publishers of the Editions of the "Christian Year" issued with the sanction and under the direction of the Author's representatives. All Editions without their imprint are unauthorized.

SMALL 4to. EDITION.
Handsomely printed on toned paper, with red border lines and initial letters. Cloth extra . . 10 6

DEMY 8vo. EDITION.
Cloth 6 0

FOOLSCAP 8vo. EDITION.
Cloth 3 6

24mo. EDITION.
Cloth, red lines 2 6

32mo. EDITION.
Cloth boards, gilt edges . . 1 6
Cloth, limp 1 0

48mo. EDITION.
Cloth, limp 0 6
Cloth boards 0 9
Roan 1 6

FACSIMILE OF THE 1st EDITION, with a list of the variations from the Original Text which the Author made in later Editions.
2 vols., 12mo., boards . . 7 6

The above Editions (except the Facsimile of the First Edition) are kept in a variety of bindings, which may be ordered through the Trade, or direct from the Publishers. The chief bindings are Morocco plain, Morocco Antique, Calf Antique, and Vellum, the prices varying according to the style.

By the same Author.

LYRA INNOCENTIUM. Thoughts in Verse on Christian Children. *Thirteenth Edition.* Fcap. 8vo., cloth, 5s.

——————— 48mo. edition, limp cloth, 6d.; cloth boards, 1s.

MISCELLANEOUS POEMS BY THE REV. JOHN KEBLE, M.A., Vicar of Hursley. [With Preface by G. M.] *Third Edition.* Fcap., cloth, 6s.

THE PSALTER, OR PSALMS OF DAVID: In English Verse. *Fourth Edition.* Fcap. cloth, 6s.

——————— 18mo., cloth, 1s.

The above may also be had in various bindings.

A CONCORDANCE TO THE "CHRISTIAN YEAR." Fcap. 8vo., toned paper, cloth, 4s.

MUSINGS ON THE "CHRISTIAN YEAR;" WITH GLEANINGS FROM THIRTY YEARS' INTERCOURSE WITH THE LATE Rev. J. KEBLE, by CHARLOTTE M. YONGE: to which are added Recollections of Hursley, by FRANCES M. WILBRAHAM. *Second Edition.* Fcap. 8vo., cloth, 7s. 6d.

MEMOIR OF THE REV. J. KEBLE, M.A. By Sir J. T. COLERIDGE. *Fourth and Cheaper Edition.* Post 8vo., cloth, 6s.

Church Poetry.

RE-ISSUE OF THE POETICAL WORKS OF THE LATE
REV. ISAAC WILLIAMS.

THE CATHEDRAL; or, The Catholic and Apostolic Church in England. Fcap. 8vo., cloth, 5s.; 32mo., cloth, 2s. 6d.

THE BAPTISTERY; or, The Way of Eternal Life. With Plates by BOETIUS A BOLSWERT. Fcap. 8vo., cloth, 7s. 6d.; 32mo., cloth, 2s. 6d.

HYMNS FROM THE PARISIAN BREVIARY. 32mo., cloth, 2s. 6d.

THE CHRISTIAN SCHOLAR. Fcap. 8vo., cl., 5s.; 32mo., cl., 2s. 6d.

THOUGHTS IN PAST YEARS. 32mo., cloth, 2s. 6d.

THE SEVEN DAYS OF THE OLD AND NEW CREATION. Fcap. 8vo., cloth, 3s. 6d.

THE CHILD'S CHRISTIAN YEAR.

THE CHILD'S CHRISTIAN YEAR. Hymns for every Sunday and Holyday throughout the Year. *Cheap Edition*, 18mo., cloth, 1s.

BISHOP CLEVELAND COXE.

CHRISTIAN BALLADS AND POEMS. By ARTHUR CLEVELAND COXE, D.D., Bishop of Western New York. A New Edition. Fcap. 8vo. cloth, 3s. Also selected Poems in a packet, 32mo., 1s.

DR. FREDERICK G. LEE.

THE BELLS OF BOTTEVILLE TOWER; A Christmas Story in Verse: and other Poems. By FREDERICK G. LEE, Author of "The Martyrs of Vienne and Lyons," "Petronilla," &c. Fcap. 8vo., with Illustrations, cloth, 4s. 6d.

Parochial.

THE CONFIRMATION CLASS-BOOK: Notes for Lessons, with APPENDIX, containing Questions and Summaries for the Use of the Candidates. By E. M. HOLMES, LL.B., Rector of Marsh Gibbon, Bucks; Diocesan Inspector of Schools; Author of the "Catechist's Manual." Fcap. 8vo., limp cloth, 2s. 6d. Also, in wrapper, THE QUESTIONS AND SUMMARIES separate, 4 sets of 128 pp. in packet, 1s. each.

THE CATECHIST'S MANUAL; with an Introduction by the late SAMUEL WILBERFORCE, D.D., Lord Bishop of Winchester. *Fifth Thousand.* Crown 8vo., limp cloth, 5s.

SHORT NOTES OF SEVEN YEARS' WORK IN A COUNTRY PARISH. By R. F. WILSON, M.A., Vicar of Rownhams, Prebendary of Sarum, and Examining Chaplain to the Bishop of Salisbury. Fcap. 8vo., cloth, 4s.

THE CHURCH AND THE SCHOOL; or, Hints on Clerical Life. By HENRY WALFORD BELLAIRS, M.A., late one of Her Majesty's Inspectors of Schools. Crown 8vo., cloth, 2s. 6d.

THE CHURCH'S WORK IN OUR LARGE TOWNS. By GEORGE HUNTINGTON, M.A., Rector of Tenby, and Domestic Chaplain of the Rt. Hon. the Earl of Crawford and Balcarres. Second Edition, revised and enlarged. Crown 8vo., cloth, 6s.

A MANUAL OF PASTORAL VISITATION, intended for the Use of the Clergy in their Visitation of the Sick and Afflicted. By a PARISH PRIEST. Dedicated, by permission, to His Grace the Archbishop of Dublin. Second Edition, Crown 8vo., limp cloth, 3s. 6d.; roan, 4s.

THE CURE OF SOULS. By the Rev. G. ARDEN, M.A., Rector of Winterborne-Came, and Author of "Breviates from Holy Scripture," &c. Fcap. 8vo., cloth, 2s. 6d.

MISCELLANEOUS.

THE ELEMENTS OF PSYCHOLOGY.

THE ELEMENTS OF PSYCHOLOGY, ON THE PRINCIPLES OF BENEKE, Stated and Illustrated in a Simple and Popular Manner by Dr. G. RAUE, Professor in the Medical College, Philadelphia; Fourth Edition, considerably Altered, Improved, and Enlarged, by JOHANN GOTTLIEB DRESSLER, late Director of the Normal School at Bautzen. Translated from the German. Post 8vo., cloth, 6s.

REV. CANON GREGORY.

ARE WE BETTER THAN OUR FATHERS? or, A Comparative View of the Social Position of England at the Revolution of 1688, and at the Present Time. FOUR LECTURES delivered in St. Paul's Cathedral. By ROBERT GREGORY, M.A., Canon of St. Paul's. Crown 8vo., 2s. 6d.

REV. CANON JENKINS.

THE AGE OF THE MARTYRS; or, the First Three Centuries of the Work of the Church of our Lord and Saviour Jesus Christ. By the late Rev. J. D. JENKINS, B.D., Canon of Pieter Maritzburg; Fellow of Jesus College, Oxford. Crown 8vo., cloth, 3s. 6d.

PROFESSOR DAUBENY.

MISCELLANIES: BEING A COLLECTION OF MEMOIRS and ESSAYS ON SCIENTIFIC AND LITERARY SUBJECTS, published at Various Times, by the late CHARLES DAUBENY, M.D., F.R.S., Professor of Botany in the University of Oxford, &c. 2 vols., 8vo., cloth, £1 1s.

FUGITIVE POEMS, relating to Subjects connected with Natural History and Physical Science, Archæology, &c. Selected by the late CHARLES DAUBENY, &c. Fcap. 8vo., cl., 5s.

PROFESSOR GOLDWIN SMITH.

THE REORGANIZATION OF THE UNIVERSITY OF OXFORD. By GOLDWIN SMITH. Post 8vo., limp cloth, 2s.

LECTURES ON THE STUDY OF HISTORY. Delivered in Oxford, 1859—61. *Second Edition.* Crown 8vo., limp cloth, 3s. 6d.

IRISH HISTORY AND IRISH CHARACTER. Cheap Edition, Fcap. 8vo., sewed, 1s. 6d.

THE EMPIRE. A Series of Letters published in "The Daily News," 1862, 1863. Post 8vo., cloth, price 6s.

MRS. ALGERNON KINGSFORD.

ROSAMUNDA THE PRINCESS: An Historical Romance of the Sixth Century; the CROCUS, WATER-REED, ROSE and MARIGOLD, PAINTER OF VENICE, NOBLE LOVE, ROMANCE of a RING, and other Tales. By Mrs. ALGERNON KINGSFORD. 8vo., cloth, with Twenty-four Illustrations, 6s.

THE EXILE FROM PARADISE.

THE EXILE FROM PARADISE, translated by the Author of the "Life of S. Teresa." Fcap., cloth, 1s. 6d.

H. A. MUNRO-BUTLER-JOHNSTONE, M.P.

THE FAIR OF NIJNI-NOVGOROD. With a Map and Twelve Illustrations. By H. A. MUNRO-BUTLER-JOHNSTONE, M.P. Second Edition, Fcap. 8vo., cloth, 5s.

THE TURKS: their Character, Manners, and Institutions, as bearing on the Eastern Question. By H. A. MUNRO-BUTLER-JOHNSTONE, M.P. 8vo., sewed, 1s.

ARCHITECTURE AND ARCHÆOLOGY. 11

THE PRAYER-BOOK CALENDAR.
THE CALENDAR OF THE PRAYER-BOOK ILLUSTRATED. (Comprising the first portion of the "Calendar of the Anglican Church," with additional Illustrations, an Appendix on Emblems, &c.) With Two Hundred Engravings from Medieval Works of Art. *Sixth Thousand.* Fcap. 8vo., cl., 6s.

SIR G. G. SCOTT, F.S.A.
GLEANINGS FROM WESTMINSTER ABBEY. By SIR GEORGE GILBERT SCOTT, R.A., F.S.A. With Appendices supplying Further Particulars, and completing the History of the Abbey Buildings, by Several Writers. *Second Edition*, enlarged, containing many new Illustrations by O. Jewitt and others. Medium 8vo., 10s. 6d.

THE LATE CHARLES WINSTON.
AN INQUIRY INTO THE DIFFERENCE OF STYLE OBSERVABLE IN ANCIENT GLASS PAINTINGS, especially in England, with Hints on Glass Painting, by the late CHARLES WINSTON. With Corrections and Additions by the Author. 2 vols., Medium 8vo., cloth, £1 11s. 6d.

REV. SAMUEL LYSONS, F.S.A.
OUR BRITISH ANCESTORS: WHO AND WHAT WERE THEY? An Inquiry serving to elucidate the Traditional History of the Early Britons by means of recent Excavations, Etymology, Remnants of Religious Worship, Inscriptions, Craniology, and Fragmentary Collateral History. By the Rev. SAMUEL LYSONS, M.A., F.S.A., Rector of Rodmarton, and Perpetual Curate of St. Luke's, Gloucester. Post 8vo., cloth, 5s.

M. VIOLLET-LE-DUC.
ON MILITARY ARCHITECTURE; Translated from the French of M. VIOLLET-LE-DUC. By M. MACDERMOTT, Esq., Architect. With the 151 original French Engravings. Medium 8vo., cloth, 10s 6d.

JOHN HEWITT.
ANCIENT ARMOUR AND WEAPONS IN EUROPE. By JOHN HEWITT, Member of the Archæological Institute of Great Britain. Vols. II. and III., comprising the Period from the Fourteenth to the Seventeenth Century, completing the work, £1 12s. Also Vol. I., from the Iron Period of the Northern Nations to the end of the Thirteenth Century, 18s. The work complete, 3 vols., 8vo., £2 10s.

REV. PROFESSOR STUBBS.
THE TRACT "DE INVENTIONE SANCTÆ CRUCIS NOSTRÆ IN MONTE ACUTO ET DE DUCTIONE EJUSDEM APUD WALTHAM," now first printed from the Manuscript in the British Museum, with Introduction and Notes by WILLIAM STUBBS, M.A. Royal 8vo., 5s.; Demy 8vo., 3s. 6d.

NORTHERN ANTIQUITIES.
THE PRIMEVAL ANTIQUITIES of ENGLAND and DENMARK COMPARED. By J. J. A. WORSAAE. Translated and applied to the illustration of similar remains in England, by W. J. THOMS, F.S.A., &c. With numerous Illustrations. 8vo., cloth, 5s.

OUR ENGLISH HOME:
Its Early History and Progress. With Notes on the Introduction of Domestic Inventions. New Edition, Crown 8vo., cloth, 3s. 6d.

JOHN HENRY PARKER, C.B., F.S.A., HON. M.A. OXON.

AN INTRODUCTION TO THE STUDY OF GOTHIC ARCHITECTURE. *Fourth Edition*, Revised and Enlarged, with 189 Illustrations, with a Topographical and Glossarial Index. Fcap. 8vo., cloth, 5s.

A CONCISE GLOSSARY OF TERMS USED IN GRECIAN, ROMAN, ITALIAN, AND GOTHIC ARCHITECTURE. A New Edition, revised. Fcap. 8vo., with 470 Illustrations, in ornamental cloth, 7s. 6d.

AN ATTEMPT TO DISCRIMINATE THE STYLES OF ARCHITECTURE IN ENGLAND, from the Conquest to the Reformation; with a Sketch of the Grecian and Roman Orders. By the late THOMAS RICKMAN, F.S.A. *Seventh Edition*, with considerable Additions, chiefly Historical, by JOHN HENRY PARKER, F.S.A., Hon. M.A. Oxon., and numerous Illustrations by O. Jewitt. 8vo. [*In the Press.*

DOMESTIC ARCHITECTURE OF THE MIDDLE AGES, with numerous Engravings from Existing Remains, and Historical Illustrations from Contemporary Manuscripts. By the late T. HUDSON TURNER, Esq. From the Norman Conquest to the Thirteenth Century; interspersed with Remarks on Domestic Manners during the same Period. 8vo., cloth, £1 1s. *A Reprint.*

——————— FROM EDWARD I. TO RICHARD II. (the Edwardian Period, or the Decorated Style). By the Editor of "The Glossary of Architecture." 8vo., cloth, £1 1s.

Also,

——————— FROM RICHARD II. TO HENRY VIII. (or the Perpendicular Style). With numerous Illustrations of Existing Remains from Original Drawings. In Two Vols., 8vo., £1 10s.

THE ARCHITECTURAL ANTIQUITIES OF THE CITY OF WELLS. By JOHN HENRY PARKER, F.S.A., Hon. M.A. Oxon., Honorary Member of the Somerset Archæological Society, &c. Illustrated by Plans and Views. Medium 8vo., cloth, 5s.

THE ARCHÆOLOGY OF ROME. By JOHN HENRY PARKER, C.B.
Part 7. THE COLOSSEUM. 8vo., Illustrated with 36 Plates, cloth, 10s. 6d.
Part 8. THE AQUEDUCTS OF ANCIENT ROME. 36 Plates, Maps, and Plans. 8vo., cloth, 15s.
Part 11. CHURCH AND ALTAR DECORATIONS IN ROME, including Mosaic Pictures and Cosmati Work. With 20 Plates and numerous Diagrams. 8vo., cloth, 10s. 6d.

SEPULCHRAL CROSSES.

A MANUAL for the STUDY of SEPULCHRAL SLABS and CROSSES of the MIDDLE AGES. By the Rev. EDWARD L. CUTTS, B.A. Illustrated by upwards of 300 Engravings. 8vo., cloth, 6s.

MEDIÆVAL IRONWORK.

SERRURERIE DU MOYEN-AGE. Par RAYMOND BORDEAUX. Forty Lithographic Plates, by G. Bouet, and numerous Woodcuts. Small 4to., cloth, £1.

MEDIÆVAL BRASSES.

A MANUAL OF MONUMENTAL BRASSES. Comprising an Introduction to the Study of these Memorials, and a List of those remaining in the British Isles. With Two Hundred Illustrations. By the late Rev. HERBERT HAINES, M.A., of Exeter College, Oxford. 2 vols., 8vo., cloth, 12s.

ENGLISH COUNTRY HOUSES.

SIXTY-ONE VIEWS AND PLANS of recently erected Mansions, Private Residences, Parsonage-Houses, Farm-Houses, Lodges, and Cottages; with Sketches of Furniture and Fittings: and A Practical Treatise on House-Building. By WILLIAM WILKINSON, Architect, Oxford. Second Edition, Royal 8vo., ornamental cloth, £1 5s.

THE ANNALS OF ENGLAND. An Epitome of English History. From Cotemporary Writers, the Rolls of Parliament, and other Public Records. A LIBRARY EDITION, revised and enlarged, with additional Woodcuts: with a Recommendatory Note by the Regius Professor of Modern History, Oxford. 8vo., half-bound, 12s.

A CONTINUATION of the above, from the Accession of George I. to the Present Time. [*In preparation.*

THE SCHOOL EDITION OF THE ANNALS OF ENGLAND. In Five Half-crown Parts. 1. Britons, Romans, Saxons, Normans. 2. The Plantagenets. 3. The Tudors. 4. The Stuarts. 5. The Restoration, to the Death of Queen Anne. Fcap. 8vo., cloth.

THE NEW SCHOOL-HISTORY OF ENGLAND, from Early Writers and the National Records. By the Author of "The Annals of England." *Sixth Thousand.* Crown 8vo., with Four Maps, limp cloth, 5s.; Coloured Maps, half roan, 6s.

A HISTORY OF THE ENGLISH CHURCH from its Foundation to the Reign of Queen Mary. By MARY CHARLOTTE STAPLEY. Third Edition, Revised, with a Recommendatory Notice by Dean Hook. Crown 8vo., cloth boards, 5s.

POETARUM SCENICORUM GRÆCORUM, Æschyli, Sophoclis, Euripidis, et Aristophanis, Fabulæ, Superstites, et Perditarum Fragmenta. Ex recognitione GUIL. DINDORFII. Editio Quinta. Royal 8vo., cloth, £1 1s.

THUCYDIDES, with Notes, chiefly Historical and Geographical. By the late T. ARNOLD, D.D. With Indices by the Rev. R. P. G. TIDDEMAN. *Eighth Edition.* 3 vols., 8vo., cloth lettered, £1 16s.

JELF'S GREEK GRAMMAR.—A Grammar of the Greek Language, chiefly from the text of Raphael Kühner. By WM. EDW. JELF, B.D., late Student and Censor of Ch. Ch. *Fourth Edition, with Additions and Corrections.* 2 vols. 8vo., £1 10s.

LAWS OF THE GREEK ACCENTS. By JOHN GRIFFITHS, D.D., Warden of Wadham College, Oxford. *Sixteenth Edition.* 16mo., price 6d.

RUDIMENTARY RULES, with Examples, for the Use of Beginners in Greek Prose Composition. By JOHN MITCHINSON, D.C.L., late Head Master of the King's School, Canterbury, (now Bishop of Barbados). 16mo., sewed, 1s.

TWELVE RUDIMENTARY RULES FOR LATIN PROSE COMPOSITION: with Examples and Exercises, for the use of Beginners. By the Rev. E. MOORE, D.D., Principal of St. Edmund Hall, Oxford. *Second Edit.* 16mo., 6d.

MADVIG'S LATIN GRAMMAR. A Latin Grammar for the Use of Schools. By Professor MADVIG, with additions by the Author. Translated by the Rev. G. WOODS, M.A. *New Edition, with an Index of Authors.* 8vo., cloth, 12s.

ERASMI COLLOQUIA SELECTA: Arranged for Translation and Re-translation; adapted for the Use of Boys who have begun the Latin Syntax. By EDWARD C. LOWE, D.D., Head Master of S. John's Middle School, Hurstpierpoint. Fcap. 8vo., strong binding, 3s.

PORTA LATINA: A Selection from Latin Authors, for Translation and Re-Translation; arranged in a Progressive Course, as an Introduction to the Latin Tongue. By EDWARD C. LOWE, D.D., Head Master of Hurstpierpoint School; Editor of Erasmus' "Colloquies," &c. Fcap. 8vo., strongly bound, 3s.

A GRAMMATICAL ANALYSIS OF THE HEBREW PSALTER; being an Explanatory Interpretation of Every Word contained in the Book of Psalms, intended chiefly for the Use of Beginners in the Study of Hebrew. By JOANA JULIA GRESWELL. Post 8vo., cloth, 6s.

SUNDAY-SCHOOL EXERCISES, Collected and Revised from Manuscripts of Burghclere School-children, under the teaching of the Rev. W. B. BARTER, late Rector of Highclere and Burghclere; Edited by his Son-in-law, the BISHOP OF ST. ANDREW'S. *Second Edition.* Crown 8vo., cloth, 5s.

A FIRST LOGIC BOOK, by D. P. CHASE, M.A., Principal of St. Mary Hall, Oxford. Small 4to., sewed, 3s.

A SERIES OF GREEK AND LATIN CLASSICS
FOR THE USE OF SCHOOLS.

GREEK POETS.

	Cloth. s. d.		Cloth. s. d.
Æschylus	3 0	Sophocles	3 0
Aristophanes. 2 vols.	6 0	Homeri Ilias	3 6
Euripides. 3 vols.	6 6	—— Odyssea	3 0
—— Tragœdiæ Sex	3 6		

GREEK PROSE WRITERS.

	s. d.		s. d.
Aristotelis Ethica	2 0	Thucydides. 2 vols.	5 0
Demosthenes de Corona, et } Æschines in Ctesiphontem }	2 0	Xenophontis Memorabilia	1 4
		—— Anabasis	2 0
Herodotus. 2 vols.	6 0		

LATIN POETS.

	s. d.		s. d.
Horatius	2 0	Lucretius	2 0
Juvenalis et Persius	1 6	Phædrus	1 4
Lucanus	2 6	Virgilius	2 6

LATIN PROSE WRITERS.

	s. d.		s. d.
Cæsaris Commentarii, cum Supplementis Auli Hirtii et aliorum	2 6	Ciceronis Tusc. Disp. Lib. V.	2 0
		Ciceronis Orationes Selectæ	3 6
—— Commentarii de Bello Gallico	1 6	Cornelius Nepos	1 4
		Livius. 4 vols.	6 0
Cicero De Officiis, de Senectute, et de Amicitia	2 0	Sallustius	2 0
		Tacitus. 2 vols.	5 0

TEXTS WITH SHORT NOTES.
UNIFORM WITH THE SERIES OF "OXFORD POCKET CLASSICS."

GREEK WRITERS. TEXTS AND NOTES.

SOPHOCLES.

	s. d.		s. d.
AJAX (*Text and Notes*)	1 0	ANTIGONE (*Text and Notes*)	1 0
ELECTRA ,,	1 0	PHILOCTETES ,,	1 0
ŒDIPUS REX ,,	1 0	TRACHINIÆ ,,	1 0
ŒDIPUS COLONEUS ,,	1 0		

The Notes only, in one vol., cloth, 3s.

ÆSCHYLUS.

	s. d.		s. d.
PERSÆ (*Text and Notes*)	1 0	CHOEPHORÆ (*Text and Notes*)	1 0
PROMETHEUS VINCTUS ,,	1 0	EUMENIDES ,,	1 0
SEPTEM CONTRA THEBAS ,,	1 0	SUPPLICES ,,	1 0
AGAMEMNON ,,	1 0		

The Notes only, in one vol., cloth, 3s. 6d.

ARISTOPHANES.

THE KNIGHTS (*Text and Notes*)	1 0	ACHARNIANS (*Text and Notes*)	1 0
THE BIRDS (*Text and Notes*)	1 0		

EURIPIDES.

	s. d.		s. d.
HECUBA (*Text and Notes*)	1 0	PHŒNISSÆ (*Text and Notes*)	1 0
MEDEA ,,	1 0	ALCESTIS ,,	1 0
ORESTES ,,	1 0	The above, Notes only, in one vol., cloth, 3s.	
HIPPOLYTUS ,,	1 0	BACCHÆ ,,	1 0

DEMOSTHENES.

DE CORONA (*Text and Notes*) . 2 0	OLYNTHIAC ORATIONS . 1 0

HOMERUS.   XENOPHON.

ILIAS, LIB. I.—VI. (*Text and Notes*) . . . 2 0	MEMORABILIA (*Text and Notes*) 2 6

ÆSCHINES.   ARISTOTLE.

IN CTESIPHONTEM (*Text and Notes*) . . . 2 0	DE ARTE POETICA (*Text and Notes*) . cloth, 2s.; sewed 1 6
	DE RE PUBLICA ,, 3s. ,, 2 6

LATIN WRITERS.   TEXTS AND NOTES.

VIRGILIUS.

BUCOLICA (*Text and Notes*)	1 0	ÆNEIDOS, LIB. I.—III. (*Text and Notes*) . . . 1 0
GEORGICA ,,	2 0	

HORATIUS.

CARMINA, &c. (*Text and Notes*)	2 0	EPISTOLÆ ET ARS POETICA (*Text and Notes*) . . . 1 0
SATIRÆ ,,	1 0	

The Notes only, in one vol., cloth, 2s.

SALLUSTIUS.

JUGURTHA (*Text and Notes*) . 1 6	CATILINA (*Text and Notes*) . 1 0

M. T. CICERO.

IN Q. CÆCILIUM — DIVINATIO (*Text and Notes*) . . 1 0	IN CATILINAM . . 1 0
IN VERREM ACTIO PRIMA . 1 0	PRO PLANCIO (*Text and Notes*) . 1 6
	PRO MILONE . . . 1 0
PRO LEGE MANILIA, et PRO ARCHIA . . . 1 0	PRO ROSCIO . . . 1 0
	ORATIONES PHILIPPICÆ, I., II. 1 6

The above, Notes only, in one vol., cloth, 3s. 6d.

DE SENECTUTE et DE AMICITIA 1 0	EPISTOLÆ SELECTÆ. Pars I. 1 6

CÆSAR.   CORNELIUS NEPOS.

DE BELLO GALLICO, LIB. I.—III. (*Text and Notes*) . . . 1 0	LIVES (*Text and Notes*) . . 1 6

LIVIUS.   PHÆDRUS.

LIB. XXI.—XXIV. (*Text and Notes*)		FABULÆ (*Text and Notes*) . 1 0
sewed 4 0		TACITUS.
Ditto in cloth . . . 4 6		THE ANNALS. Notes only, 2 vols., 16mo., cloth . . . 7 0

Portions of several other Authors are in preparation.

Uniform with the Oxford Pocket Classics.

THE LIVES OF THE MOST EMINENT ENGLISH POETS; WITH CRITICAL OBSERVATIONS ON THEIR WORKS. By SAMUEL JOHNSON. 3 vols., 24mo., cloth, 2s. 6d. each.

THE LIVES OF ADDISON, DRYDEN, AND POPE, with Critical Observations on their Works. By SAMUEL JOHNSON. With Analyses of the Lives. 24mo., cloth, 2s.

CHOICE EXTRACTS FROM MODERN FRENCH AUTHORS, for the use of Schools. 18mo., cloth, 3s.

BOOKS, &c., RELATING TO OXFORD.

A HANDBOOK FOR VISITORS TO OXFORD. Illustrated with Woodcuts by Jewitt, and Steel Plates by Le Keux. *A New Edition.* 8vo., cloth, 12s.

THE OXFORD UNIVERSITY CALENDAR for 1877. Corrected to the end of December, 1876. 12mo., cloth, 4s. 6d.

THE OXFORD TEN-YEAR BOOK: A Complete Register of University Honours and Distinctions, made up to the end of the Year 1870. Crown 8vo., roan, 7s. 6d.

PASS AND CLASS: An Oxford Guide-Book through the Courses of *Literæ Humaniores*, Mathematics, Natural Science, &c. By MONTAGU BURROWS, Chichele Professor of Modern History. *Third Edition.* Revised and Enlarged; with Appendices on the Indian Civil Service, the Diplomatic Service, and the Local Examinations. Fcap. 8vo., cloth, price 2s.

THE OXFORD UNIVERSITY EXAMINATION PAPERS.

Printed directly from the Examiners' Copies.

EXAMINATION PAPERS, First Public, IN DISCIPLINIS MATHEMATICIS. From 1863 to 1873. Selection of 12 Papers. Cloth, 7s. 6d.

———————————— Second Public, IN SCIENTIIS MATHEMATICIS ET PHYSICIS. From 1863 to 1873. Selection of 12 Papers. Cloth, 7s. 6d.

———————————— in the School of NATURAL SCIENCE. From 1863 to 1868. Complete, 12 Papers, cloth, 7s. 6d.

——— From 1868 to 1873. Complete, 10 Papers, cloth, 6s.

———————————— in the School of LAW AND MODERN HISTORY. From 1867 to 1872. Complete, 12 Papers, cloth, 7s. 6d.

Many of the Examination Papers contained in the above volumes may be had separately at 1s. *each. Also the Papers in the Schools of* THEOLOGY, MODERN HISTORY, *and* JURISPRUDENCE *for* 1872 *and* 1873, *price* 1s. *each.*

UNIVERSITY OF OXFORD LOCAL EXAMINATIONS. Examination Papers and Division Lists for the years 1860 and 1861. 8vo., *each* 3s. 6d.

——— Examination Papers for the years 1870, 1871, 1872, 1873, 1874, 1875, 1876, *each* 2s.

——— Division Lists for the years 1867, 1868, *each* 1s. 6d.

——————— for the years 1869, 1870, 1871, 1872, 1873, 1874, 1875, 1876, *each* 2s.

www.ingramcontent.com/pod-product-compliance
Lightning Source LLC
Chambersburg PA
CBHW031959230426
43672CB00010B/2207